THE RED LEATHER CHAIR

Ingrid Kraus

Cover Design: Adam Tiller

Published by Wry Hill

ISBN 13:978-0615723709
ISBN 10:0615723705

For Jeff

Who dares and cares.

To every thing there is a season . . .

Ecclesiastes 3:1

SPRING

Chapter 1

JONAH

He invited Dawn to sit in his red leather chair.

"So why don't you take off your shoes," my husband, Deal, said. "Get comfortable."

"Get comfortable?" I said. "Get comfortable?"

At Deal's invitation, Dawn looked at me with her head slightly cocked and settled herself into the chair. She looked down at her backless tennis shoes and lightly kicked off first one, then the other.

"This would be a cushy life, she said." She smiled at me from the red leather chair and wriggled her bare toes. They were painted an iridescent light pink color like the inside of a seashell. Her long blond hair shimmered each time a breeze blew my lace curtains into the room.

"This *would* be a cushy life," she repeated and scanned the living room like she was taking inventory.

When Deal issued his invitation, my grandson Danny and I were playing horsey and galumphing along on the oval braided rug in front of the fireplace. I bucked Danny a little too hard, and he dug his tiny heels into my ribs and choked my neck so as not to take a tumble. I unclenched his sweet fingers. Maybe I gasped, but I didn't cry out. Children should not suffer from the foolishness of adults.

Dawn, wife of my second son, Wally, had taken to dropping by in the late afternoons, right about the hour Deal, my husband of thirty years, took his break. I just thought Dawn was bored around this time of day. Wally often worked late, so it was too soon to start supper, and her day's chores were probably mostly done.

After Dawn left and I fed Danny and his two brothers whom I was babysitting, I approached Deal in the living room. He was ensconced in the red leather chair reading the evening paper. I was burping the baby, a cloth diaper on my shoulder.

Although neither I nor my four children nor their children had ever been allowed to sit in the red leather chair, I knew exactly how it felt. The top of the back arched like a rainbow to give you height. The plush padding provided support. Mainly, though, the regal bearing of the chair taught you—that you were important. Once you found such a simple route to an inner sense of your value in this world, you would be lost to the pull of the chair forever.

"Look, Deal," I said. "I will not stand for this sort of humiliation. What is your meaning here? Inviting Dawn to sit in your chair when it's been off limits to anyone but you for thirty years? If this ever happens again, I, I will resign."

"Resignation accepted," Deal said studying the pattern in the oval rug, the blues and grays going round and round.

"Resignation accepted? As simple as that after I've raised four children. Resignation accepted?"

"You heard me. Resignation accepted." Deal set the paper down and went out to find a chore to keep him company.

Danny poked his head in from the kitchen. I set the baby in his car seat, scooped Danny up and hugged him hard. Maybe a tear escaped me. I cleared the kids' dishes off the kitchen table and sponged the oilcloth. It had a few torn places.

Danny's mom, Manya, wife of my third son, arrived not long after, finished with her shopping.

"Jonah." She hugged me and spread her purchases out.

"Cute, no? Funny me. I leaving the kids five minutes, and I missing them so."

She showed me with her hands on her heart. She is a big woman, and she has a big heart.

"Look. A new blanket for Toto. He growing, growing. And a little horse for Danny. Why he love horses so much, Jonah? And—how you say—boxers for Vanya, my big boy."

Manya is my Russian daughter-in-law, but her warmth knows no nationality.

That night, I packed Deal's bags, folding his shirts to look as though I'd just picked them up at Penney's.

He woke up and saw four suitcases there by the bed, one for each child we had together, and he hit the roof.

"I meant for you to go," he said.

"I know what you meant," I said.

Deal put those suitcases in his pickup. He came back in and hoisted up the red leather armchair with the high padded back, wrapped it in some plastic sheeting he must have found in the barn, put it on its side in the double cab behind the driver's seat and took off.

When I tried to walk, the air had thickness and didn't give way like it usually does. The best I could do was sit down, but the living room seemed empty without that ridiculous red armchair, so I went into the family room. It seemed like a miracle that a person could still breathe when the air was so thick.

My daughter-in-law Dawn was beautiful, to be sure, with her long, glistening blond hair. You could get lost watching the light play on her hair the way you get lost watching a fire in the fireplace.

Still to me, she was like an outline waiting to be filled in—almost like a ghost. She was so young, of course, and undefined. But the funny thing was, when I thought about it, I felt the same way. Who was I after all? A woman of fifty-four with a pleasant round face who had raised four children and had a husband who lived inside a red leather chair. What was inside my outline really?

I went to a psychiatrist. He had a voice with a frog in it like John Wayne's —kind of guttural but sticky sweet at the same time. He said, "It's good to do things differently from time to time," as though losing your husband and his red leather chair to your daughter-in-law was like deciding one morning to drink your coffee in the shower.

When I went home, I looked through my husband's side of the closet—empty, of course, since I'd emptied it myself. Then I looked at my side. Still full. Full of ancient, worn dresses. And lo and behold, one of his two suits hung there in error, still in the cleaner's wrapping. I poked my finger through the clear, thin plastic. "Go for it, moths," I said. "Go for it."

Chapter 2

DANIEL

Manya and I had been concerned about my mom and dad's relationship for some time. It certainly didn't seem to have much zip in it, as Manya, my wife, likes to say. She loves to practice American slang with her Russian accent. God, she's cute, well, not exactly cute. She's tall, about 5'10", and broad-shouldered. She's a generous-sized woman. God, I love her, every one of her big Russian bones.

The day before Deal actually left the farmhouse, Manya had dropped the kids off at Mama's to do some shopping. When they got home, later in the afternoon, I was back from teaching and two committee meetings and was kind of droopy. I was vaguely thumbing through a cookbook, wondering whether something in the fridge could be turned into dinner.

"Daniel!" said Danny, my middle child, running over and hugging my leg. For some reason, Danny often calls me Daniel instead of Dad or Daddy. And he says my name so seriously, like we are having a colloquium on historiographical thought. It always makes me want to hug him even if I am driving or shaving or whatever, which, of course, can be impractical.

"Hey, Danny." I whirled him around carefully so as not to hit the onions I'd set on the counter.

"Daniel," he said in his solemn tone, "why was *Babushka* crying?"

Babushka is the Russian word for grandmother. Manya, my wife, uses that word, and I guess Danny's picked it up.

Obviously, he has. Manya hugged our Danny and asked, "Why, Danilushka, you think Babushka was crying?"

"Because she was wiping her eyes with tissoo," Danny said.

He's four, and still has his mouth full of his words now and then. Plus, maybe his mother's accent confuses him at times.

"Did she get something in her eye, Danny boy?" I asked, hoping for the non-emotional, professorial approach.

"I didn't see a little fly, Daniel," he said. "I was looking. I a good boy." He smiled at me, his face upturned.

"You're my best boy," I said.

"No, I not. We is all your best boys, Toto and Ivan and Danny."

Toto, that's Arthur's nickname. He's my youngest. He's 8 months. Ivan is eight.

"For sure, Danilushka," I said to Danny, squatting down on the floor next to him. "Toto and Ivan and Danny and Mama and Papa are all the best family anybody could ever have in this world. But what happened to Babushka?"

"I not know. Auntie Dawn sitted in *Dedushka's* chair. Babushka said she resign. Dedushka said something. Then Babushka using the tissoo. What is 'resign'?"

"Gee, little buddy," I looked at Manya for help, "usually it means you want to quit your job."

"Is Babushka going to quit her job, Daniel?"

"We not know, Danilushka," Manya said. "We finding out, okay?"

MANYA

I tell Daniel not worry, I go tomorrow seeing Jonah. I take boys after Ivan getting out of school and Danny getting out of preschool. Daniel say okay. He wish he go too but have to teach.

We living not so far from mother of Daniel, maybe one and one-half hours for driving, and she love to seeing boys always.

She a good grandmother. She their babushka.

My mother been here when Danilushka and Toto born. My father not feeling good for traveling. I was coming to States after my husband die in Chechnya. *Bozhe moi.* I bringing my little Ivan, my Vanya, and I thinking to working hard and making better life in new country. Is long story. I very lucky. I finding good man with zip.

We going in Jonah's house, and Jonah sitting. Looking like she maybe crying. The boys running and hugging their babushka. I go hugging her too. Then she definitely crying, bozhe moi, and I send boys outside to playing.

"Sorry, Manya," she say to me.

"No sorry, no sorry. What is problem?" I asking.

"Oh, Manya," she say and go to cry again.

I finding tissoo and giving.

She tell me not a good story. She telling me she bad wife, bad lady. I no understand. She so a good lady. She say Deal go away, and I start to crying too. No is good, so I stop to crying.

"But why?" I asking her.

"I'm not sure, Manya," she saying.

She no want to say. She want to protect Deal. Deal is good man too, she saying.

"Deal's a good man, Manya."

I see her hold tissoo tight, tight. "*Da, da,*" I say. "Deal a good man."

Chapter 3

JONAH

When Deal was a boy, his father took him to the circus. The tiger was misbehaving that day in rehearsal, so they scrapped the wild animal part of the show. Deal had wanted to go to the circus mostly because of the wild animals and so was understandably distressed.

After the circus was over, his father, God rest his soul, took him to the outlying tents, to the cages where the wild animals were kept, so Deal could at least take a look at them. The trainer was sitting next to the cages smoking a cigarette in a long gold cigarette holder. Whenever Deal told me about it, he'd emphasize the *gold* part and the *long* part. It must have been a heck of a cigarette holder.

And, of course, the trainer was sitting in a red leather armchair with a tall padded back.

He had wonderful pantaloons with silver and gold stripes on them, and his muscles loomed like mountains on his bare chest. You'd have to think that right there with the animal smells and the performers half-dressed and unwinding after the show, and the cooks speaking some kind of gibberish and the clowns without their faces, Virility was screaming out at Deal, "This is what it means to grow up, son. You too can be a wild animal trainer or tamer" or some such as that.

Years later, when Deal and I were out looking for bunk beds for the first two kids because the third one was coming along nicely, Deal spotted a tall padded red leather armchair in the furniture store, and he just had to have it. Never mind that we were young and struggling, me with stretching his income to fill up four-and-a-half hungry people, and him with working way too much, growing feed corn and soybeans and hassling with corn borers and rootworm larvae and the grain elevators. Never mind that our extra pennies were kept in a jar not a bank vault. Never mind that making a baby was sometimes the best we could do for affection. He had to have that chair. I put it on layaway, and by Christmas, I made certain I had that damn chair under the tree for him with a ribbon with silver and gold stripes tied around it slantwise, like Miss America's sash.

He nearly died. He hugged me so hard, off and on all day long. The grin would not leave his face. I got sick of seeing his teeth. But, truly, I was so glad for him. And he played with the kids all day and never lost his patience with them even once. And I thought—silly me—that nothing could ever stop us now, not one thing.

DEAL

I plow dirt. My crops feed on dirt. And my cattle are raised on the bluestem grasses that grow on dirt. Course, I don't actually plow dirt. It's soil, and mighty rich soil at that. It kind of skims the Flint Hills of Kansas, near where I live. Can't get too deep. Too rocky. But rich, mighty rich. You have to burn the weeds off every year. Deliberately set a prairie fire to make room for the new grass. Gets so green after that burning…it'll put your eyes out.

My farm was handed down to me from generations of Strayhorns who tried to love the land. Some years, the earth was so parched and cracked, it would trap a wagon wheel.

Some years, mud. Some years, chinch bugs that sucked the juices out of feed corn. Many a hard-working man fed his stock with that ruined crop, not realizing. Then he'd find them, one by one, dying of starvation. Hard to imagine what that does to a man who's tried to do right by his animals. Kind of like watching your children wither before your very eyes. A piece of you dries up inside with the helplessness of it.

Whether the land wanted to nourish us or not, I wanted to feed my family, and feed them I did. Ah, but how? There's the rub. I was like most of my fellow men, farmers and ranchers all. We got seduced by mechanization and by keeping up with the Joneses. I'd say there were times I was even competing with my ancestors. What kind of person pays attention to the imagined opinions of dead people? Produce more, produce better. You can't stop until you're so tired all you can do is sit and watch TV. You lose sight of the family you're working to feed. They lose sight of you.

Of our four kids, three keep their hands clean. But I have one son who pokes around in the dirt: mighty proud of my oldest boy, Field. He's a dirt fellow like his dad. Course, he's a contractor. Has to break ground for new construction. Well, I guess even Daniel, he's my third son—gonna' be a prof with a Ph.D.—even Daniel sifts through the dust of history. I suppose they both got it from me. My other two, Wally and Anna, are not dirt people, but Anna at least has a prairie fire in her. Wally, I don't know. He's not like the rest of us. Sometimes, I wonder where he came from...if he's really my son. When he was just a little boy, he had to come in the kitchen and wash his hands off if they got the least bit of dirt on them. If I said, "Wally, a little dirt won't kill you," he would scowl and pummel me. Hot-tempered from the git-go. I had a knack for setting him off, and then he'd cry. Jonah would put her arms around him and protect him from me. From *me.* She coddled that boy. Mollycoddled. And he preferred her. A mama's boy. The others—they seemed to take more of a shine to me: followed me around, wanted to show me their scribblings. Even Daniel—well, at least he cottoned to both of us.

Sunday morning, Dawn met me at the apartment I'd rented. I'd been there about a week and managed to buy some pots and pans and a dinette set. Also a bed.

After she called and told me she was coming over in the morning, I didn't sleep a wink. I was hyperventilating, and my fingers started to tingle. About every half second, a different place under my skin started to itch. I turned on the light and looked at the new sheets to see if they'd gotten bedbugs somehow. I looked all over for a paper bag to breathe into to calm myself down. There were some plastic grocery bags. No paper ones. What the hell was I doing?

She rang the doorbell, and the minute I saw her, it was like veils or scales or whatever fell from my eyes, and I knew I'd made the worst mistake of my life.

"So you really meant it when you said you were coming over this morning?" I took the suitcase she was holding. Well, come in then, Dawn. Make yourself at home. Can I fix you some breakfast?"

"Oh, would you?" she asked. "I slipped out so early, I haven't had a morsel. I'm just famished."

"Famished," I repeated, steadying myself on the kitchen counter. I had eggs and bacon. I could cook toast in the broiler. I had butter and jelly. Salt. I think I forgot to get any salt.

Here was this child, all that long, golden hair, yes, but a child, really, about the same age as my Anna, and I was supposed to enfold her in my arms and start a life with her. I was supposed to have carried her across this new threshold. I was supposed to sleep with her, for God's sake. There was no way that was going to be even remotely possible. I'd be a child molester. Well, of course, she was of age, and that hair was aching to be stroked…ever so gently. But me, I would feel like I was taking advantage. My fingers are thick and bristly. The dark, wavy hair on my head is thinning. You could see my scalp through it in places. I've always been a handsome guy, I think, but my face is permanently tanned and lined. Only fifty-five, though. Not bad for fifty-five.

"I think I forgot to get salt," I said. "Eggs without salt. Not great." I was still holding her suitcase with one hand and the counter with the other. I set the suitcase down.

"We could just go grab a bite somewhere." She smiled.

"Uh," I said. "I haven't shaved yet. Let's just eat here this morning. Who needs salt?"

She moved closer, and I could smell that musky smell again. It was all over the red leather chair from before like the pollen dust from lilies.

"Dawn," I said, "I'm not so sure this is a good idea, actually," I said.

"Oh," she said, "not sure, huh?"

She didn't back away. She had a very soft voice. Hard to hear.

Chapter 4

WALLY

I reached out for Dawn before opening my eyes to the bright light forcing its way around the edges of her floral drapes. My hand touched the sheet. "Dawn," I called. No answer. Maybe she went out to get milk. Or coffee. Maybe she went out for a walk.

I got up, put on my bathrobe, and padded around the house, peering into the two bathrooms. It wasn't like her to wake early. I was the early bird. She normally liked to lounge on a weekend. I'd bring her coffee and the paper in bed. Later, after she'd had her bath, I'd fix a hearty breakfast. Tell the truth, she might lounge around some on the weekdays too. She didn't always have a job to go to. I made enough, though. I could support both of us.

No Dawn. Car was gone, purse gone, so not just out for a walk. No note. She wasn't much of a note writer. Lots of times, even if I were just going to work, I'd write her a love note in the morning before I left. Usually, something silly like, "Roses are red, violets are blue, you're my honey, and you sure are sweet."

Hmm, wonder where she went. Probably to the store. I crawled back into bed intending to nap a few more minutes, but her open closet door caught my eye. It was empty. I must have done a double take before a shiver running through my body from my head to my toes and back up to my head again caught up with my brain. No! Why was her closet bare?

I hauled on my clothes without buttoning my shirt or tying my shoes. I grabbed my wallet and my keys, and I went to the liquor cabinet and belted down a couple swigs off an open fifth of Jack Daniels. "Dawn," I called one more time. She wouldn't leave me, would she? I drained the rest of the bottle and grabbed my Glock from the drawer of my bedside table.

I drove with a kind of tunnel vision, very focused, but with no clue which direction to drive in. The whiskey didn't seem to reach the jagged edges of my nerves. I could barely tolerate sitting in the car, but what else could I do? Run all over the county? I plowed my hand through my hair and pounded on the steering wheel. "Dawn, Dawn, where the hell are you?" No answer.

I was looking for her white convertible VW bug. Had she gone home to her mother's in Kansas City? Was she still in town? What was I missing? How had I missed it? She wouldn't cheat on me, would she?

Then I saw it. It was parked in front of a building in an apartment complex. I squealed to a stop in front of her car, got out, and scanned the area. "What the fuck, Dawn? What the fuck?" I grabbed the Glock and shot out her tires: one, two, three, four. The car poofed down to the rims. I moved to face it straight on and shot out her headlights. I was wishing I had a sharp knife to slash the convertible roof to shreds when Dad opened the front door of that apartment building. He had on a robe. "Wally," he said.

"Dad," I said, a quick shake to try to clear my head, "what are you doing here?" I saw Dawn, also in a robe, hiding behind Dad and peeking out. She looked flushed, best I could see. Then it hit me. Maybe the whiskey had, after all, slowed some of my nerves, the ones that make logical connections. I raised the gun and took aim at Deal.

Someone must have called the cops after hearing me shoot Dawn's car. Pop pop sounds outside your apartment don't usually accompany the sound of Sunday bacon frying.

I pulled the trigger on Deal, and two policemen blazed into the parking lot and tackled me from behind, karate-chopped the gun out of my hand, and stuffed me into the squad car. Soon as they got me muzzled, I passed out.

When I came to, I was in a cubicle, strapped to a gurney, and Mama was sitting by me in a chair. I saw her through a haze.

"Where am I, Mama?" My head ached.

"We're in the ER," she said. "I just got here. How are you feeling?"

"Whew," I said. "How am I feeling?"

"They said when they brought you in, you were throwing up and cursing and talking crazy, Wally. They said you pushed a nurse trying to get out of here, and they had to restrain you."

"Did I kill the son-of-a-bitch, Mama? Did I kill them both?"

"What are you talking about, Wallace? Watch your language."

"I'm talking about Dad, and I don't give a shit about my language. I don't give a shit about anything, Mama. I tried to shoot Dad. I pointed my gun at him and pulled the trigger. I think I pulled the trigger."

"Well," Mama said, and she got up and put her arm around me, "I care about your language, Wally, and I care about you. You are my dear, dear boy."

I started sobbing the way you do when you're a kid, and your first dog runs into the back wheels of a FedEx truck. Mama just held me tighter.

"I hope I killed the bastard," I said.

"Given that Deal called me and told me to meet you at the ER and never mentioned bleeding to death," Mama said quietly, "I'm guessing they're still walking around on God's green earth. Or lying on it. Or something."

JONAH

I robbed our minuscule retirement account to post Wally's bail and brought him home with me. He gave me his word that he would control himself despite his agitation over being betrayed by his wife. And his father. You think a berserk football player might be bad, it's nothing like a berserk accountant. All those years of being precise were pouring out of him.

Plus, Wally was twenty-nine by then. He and Deal had a history—or a non-history, really. Wally had always been extremely smart and really very sweet and loving, but he had always lived somewhat in the shadow of our oldest son, Mayfield, who was a brawny, impulsive, popular kid. Now I know it's usually the reverse, that the first kid is the brain, and the second kid is the brawn, but that's not how it was in our family, probably because when Field—that's what we usually call Mayfield—was little, Deal still pitched balls to him and threw a football with him and didn't just give up on living from being so plain, darn tired all the time.

We were sitting at the kitchen table, or at least I was. Wally kept popping up out of his chair. I had a bowl of fruit out, and he kept picking up an apple, tossing it back and forth from one hand to the other as he paced, and then setting it back down in the bowl kind of hard so the bananas got bruised.

"Mama," he said, "I got out the whiskey someone gave us for our wedding night, and I drained the bottle. I was rabid. I was howlin'." He made a kind of choked screeching sound and went and got a glass of water. "After that, I got my gun and went looking even though I didn't know where to start. Why didn't you tell me what was happening?"

"Oh, Wally." There was a hollow place in my chest. "I probably should have, but it was so awkward and devastating and humiliating, and I thought maybe it would pass. I never thought she'd take it far enough to move in with him. I figured she'd get sick of him quick, and you'd never have to know, maybe. I just didn't want you to have to hurt."

"Oh, Mama." He patted my shoulder and closed his eyes for a moment. "I drove around and drove around," he continued, "and since it was Sunday, and most folks were at church, the streets were pretty deserted. I didn't even know what I was looking for except maybe for her white VW bug. When I saw it in the parking lot of this apartment complex, I shot out all her tires. Then I shot out her headlights. I was about to shoot out the taillights and go find a knife to cut up the convertible roof, but somebody in the complex must have called the cops. I saw Dad, Mama. I saw Dad in a robe and Dawn was right behind him. In a robe, Mama. I aimed at Dad. I tried to kill my dad. Both of them if the bullet would go through him into her. I can't remember if I fired. I'm pretty sure I fired."

WALLY

I wish I could run their little feet off the rails. I wish I could bash their fucking heads in. I wish I could soak their bodily juices in lye and rub that concoction all over them and around them and through them 'til they burned in hell.

What is the price of humiliation? The price of humiliation is my red cheeks. On my face and my ass. Showing me their ass. Sons of bitches. I'll show them mine. I don't have to calculate assets and liabilities. I don't have to figure credits and debits. I don't have to keep any fucking columns straight. There's sex, and there's death. Period. Two plus two is four. No brainer.

They didn't have to do this. They had options. Plenty of options. I was the one who didn't have a prayer. Didn't even know I didn't have a prayer.

Sex was good between us. At least, I thought so. Dawn never complained. She'd arch like a cat and grin. Seemed like she was into it. Couldn't have been faking all the time, I don't think. So what? When? Where? How? Why? The big why. The very big why.

So I'm a regular guy. So I'm a little dull. Chartered accountant, yeah, yeah. I've got a sense of humor like the next fellow. I've got jazz in my prick. What else is there?

I took a girl out from behind a cosmetics counter. A cosmetics counter! She was a mannequin, and I gave her a life, and now she thinks it wasn't a life?

What the hell am I supposed to do next? I'm supposed to keep on keeping on. I'm supposed to be a good boy? You can fucking shove that up your bony ass, Deal Strayhorn. I was a good boy, but good ain't the word I'm fucking feeling right this moment. You can believe me. We aren't finished.

You can't spread your mayonnaise and wipe the knife off on my shirt. You can't get away with it just because you're my dad. You wouldn't allow someone to violate one of your kin, now would you? And you're the one who taught me that, didn't you: "Don't let them intimidate you, Wally. Okay, son? You're a big boy now." Damn fucking right. I'm a big boy now. I'm a man whether you and Dawn think so or not. I'll show you I'm a man.

Just 'cause I work indoors and you work outdoors, you think you rule. Well, my brain will rule your body, you son of a bitch. Forget that. I'll work out these arms 'til they can take you easy. I'll work out these legs 'til I can outrun your monster truck. Then we'll see who doesn't have a prayer.

Why'd you do it, Deal? Goddamnit. God, goddamnit, I'm on my knees to You. Why the hell did You let this happen?

DEAL

I've never been a guy who's just about sex despite my years in front of the TV. Who let humor like The Honeymooners and variety shows like Ed Sullivan and Perry Como give way to sexpots selling cars and beer anyway?

When I got back from Vietnam, I was looking around for what's next, glad to be alive. My parents were getting on. Well, they were probably as old as I am now. That's a sobering thought. The family farm was waiting. One of my buddies dared me to take Jonah out. I think he meant it to be a mean joke on Jonah, some kind of put down. After all, she hadn't really been part of the football crowd in high school, and she was still unmarried, working at the five & dime in town, taking classes at Tall Grass Community College, living at her crazy aunt's. I took her to see "The Last Movie." It had Dennis

Hopper in it. He plays a cowboy named, believe it or not, Kansas. I think that's why I wanted to see it.

I picked Jonah up in my Chevelle convertible. Those were the days. After being ten different kinds of hot and sweaty in Vietnam, I found Jonah cool and dry to the touch when I ushered her to her seat. She seemed placid. No bombs were going to go off. No land mines. No booby traps. I fell into her calm waters, I guess you could say. I didn't resurface 'til Dawn.

For several months, I'd noticed Dawn coming 'round to the house in the afternoons right when I'd take a break. Or she and Wally would come over for dinner, and while she was helping Jonah in the kitchen, I'd go in for a glass of iced tea for me and Wally, and I'd sneak a look at her. She'd be wearing something simple, cutoffs maybe, and a tee shirt, but on her they were electrically charged. If she were, say, chopping carrots and celery sticks, she'd make a point to squeeze by me as I twisted ice cubes out of the tray. The hairs on my arms would stand up.

All of a sudden, at fifty-five, I was devastated by sex, consumed by a picture in my mind of riding Dawn, her golden hair flying and alive in the moonlight. Every "accidental" touch was like a brush fire.

When we set the prairie fires every spring to burn off the weeds, it's quite a sight. Especially, at night. There's photographers who come from other states to capture the spectacle of it. You see a wall of flame coming toward you across the prairie. Of course, we take a lot of precautions before setting a fire. We make sure there's been plenty of rain. We make sure to build firebreaks. We make sure no people or animals or buildings or equipment are in the line of fire, so to speak, so no one can get hurt. I didn't take these precautions with Dawn.

I don't know how many months things went on like this. You'd have thought Wally or Jonah would have had a clue. Maybe they did, but they couldn't really admit it to themselves. It was like they were looking at one of those Van de Graaff generators they used to show us in elementary school, but they couldn't see the sparks.

One day, Dawn came over to pick up some greens from the cold frame. Jonah must have called her because we had extra and told her to help herself. Jonah was out, and I'd just come in for a tool or something. Dawn was washing the greens off in the sink. She turned and looked up at me when I walked in, and I knew I was sunk. "Deal," she said, and she moved in close to me, and I put my arms around her and kissed her all over: her face, her lips, and that goddamn hair, all over that goddamn hair. So silky under my fingers.

I tried to do right. I pulled apart from her.

And then, she said, "I'm ready, Deal. Are you?"

I remember hearing about Johnny Cash falling head-over-heels for June Carter while he was still married. Supposedly, she saved him from a life, or I guess you could say a death, of drugs and prison. Johnny Cash was a Christian, like me, and I suppose I thought if he could get away with adultery and make it turn out for the best, then so could I. The Bible says, "Thou shalt not covet thy neighbor's wife." It doesn't say anything about your son's wife.

Chapter 5

FIELD

People always remember where they were when they first hear of a disaster.

Of course, Deal's moving out can't compare to the collapse of the Twin Towers, but then you can't compare disasters in terms of how they make you feel. Emotions are rather personal. Okay, highly personal. I don't have the widest frame of reference. Other than the highs of marriage to my high school sweetheart and the births of my two kids, I just kind of rock right along. In my line of work, it pays dividends to keep emotions under wraps. I probably take after Deal in that regard.

I was at work—I own a construction company—when Deal called, and I couldn't talk right then. "I'll call you back tonight, Dad," I said. "Inspector's on the way. Gotta' meet him at the job site. Little problem brewing out there."

"Okay, son," Dad said.

"Everything okay?" I asked. He didn't call all that often.

"Fine, fine," Dad said. "Talk to you tonight.

"Son," he said when I reached him on my way home, "Um, I guess you need to know. I've moved out."

"Moved out? Moved out from where?"

"From the farm," he said.

"Are you kidding?" I asked pulling the pickup onto the shoulder, putting it into park, and wishing I could at least idle the engine revving in my heart.

"There's more, son," he said, but I could barely hear him.

"I think you're breaking up," I said. "Your phone is breaking up."

I tried calling him back, but I just got a message, so as I eased back on the road and headed toward my kid's soccer game, I called Mom. I didn't call all that often either. Take after Deal in that regard too.

"Mom," I said.

"Field," she said. "Is that you, Field? Oh, honey, how are you?"

"I'm fine, Mom," I crossed my fingers so the lie wouldn't count. How old was I anyway? "But Deal just called, and I couldn't quite understand him. His phone was breaking up. Is there something I need to know?"

"Oh, honey, I should have called you right away. Are you sitting down?"

"So it's true, is it?" I asked. "He really moved out?" My composure seemed to crack like a shoddy foundation.

"Oh, honey, I've been trying to get up the nerve to tell you."

"He said there was more." I pulled off onto the shoulder again and looked at my watch. Unclear whether I'd make it to that soccer game.

"Maybe I better tell you in person," Mom said. "Can you come over after work in the next few days?"

"That bad?" I asked.

"Well," Mom said. "Not that great."

"Tomorrow, Mom," I said. "I'll come over after work tomorrow."

DAWN

Passion is not just a fragrance.

I used to work at Dillard's in Kansas City, so I should know. We had ninety-nine fragrances. The older women, not necessarily the total geriatrics, but the ones that could relate to Elizabeth Taylor, they would ask for "Passion," and I would have to tell them, "Um, we don't carry that fragrance, ma'am, but we have ninety-nine other ones. Here let me show you." And I would flick my head so my hair would swing out in a curvy swirl like in a shampoo ad, and they'd know I was prettier than them. I would swish my butt so they would know I was getting some and they ought to pay attention to the tester bottles I was spraying on them and what all I was sayin' because they needed a little sprucing up—not. They needed a lot of sprucing up. I so liked that I had their full attention on a topic of my expertise, those teacher types that used to put me down.

Then, of course, there were the guys that came by to gawk, not just at my hair, nuh uh, pretending they had to buy a present for their girlfriend or their mother or…God, guys are so totally transparent and so easy to play. Guys are almost too easy to play. I have a low tolerance for boredom. I was so glad when they invented glue-on fingernails because I used to chew my fingernails, and I never could wait for my fingernails to grow all the way out.

I was in love once. When I was a kid, I was in love with my dad: Mister Tall, Dark and Handsome. Looked a little like Field. Funny, I didn't care that much what he looked like back then. I cared that he played with me. Everything from Monopoly to Donkey Kong to shooting baskets. He was a great dad until he left. After that, everything was just payback.

Me paying him back in spades. And how did I do that? I got a lot of spades, and I pulled them out of my sleeve, one by one. I slapped that spade down on a table. Any guy's table. Any time I felt like it.

Chapter 6

JONAH

Deal and Dawn never pressed charges, but the D.A. did, and Wally had to turn in his gun. Eventually, he got off with supervised probation, probably because he had no previous record. Maybe also because Mrs. Marshall, the D.A.'s mother, attends our church, and God knows you can count on the folks in our church to talk about these "churchly" matters, like Deal leaving and taking up with Dawn, as frequently as humanly possible.

As far as I know, Wally's never spoken to Deal or Dawn since. He busies himself with work and sometimes, he sits with me in church—we know how to hold our heads up. Lately, he's taken up canoeing and kayaking. Well, I'll be. Whoever heard of canoeing and kayaking in Kansas? But there's a whitewater club here. He started out learning how to roll his kayak on Melvern Lake and Redmond Reservoir. Now his whitewater groups go all over: the Snake, the Salmon. He looks so strong and brown, it puts a lump in my throat.

The first day he went canoeing, he saw a bald eagle. It was just sitting up in a tree.

"Mama," he said with a mouthful of mashed potatoes one Sunday after church, "you know when I saw that eagle's white head, I knew it was an omen. That bird is majestic. It looked me straight in the eye. 'Courage, Wallace,' it said. Then it dove for a fish. You have never seen anything move that fast. Flash. Zoom. Now, when I'm out canoeing, I'm checking for that bird. Keeps me going. So you see," he said, like you say when you're trying to convince yourself, "I'll be okay. I'll be fine just like that eagle. You can bank on it."

The first time Deal crawled back home, he was standing upright. He knocked on my door right when I was putting away the supper dishes. I'd fixed me a little chicken and dumplings, comfort food, for the long evening ahead. Because, truth to tell, I was fine during the days, full of my job and gifts for the grandkids, and little home repair projects, and calling on older folks from church who needed a lift, but the evenings had a way of wearing on me. I couldn't rightly get situated in that big old house with no one else in it.

The space around me echoed with memories of our dog, Fella, tumbling down the stairs when he was a gangly Irish Setter puppy or Field scarring the new linoleum with his first football cleats or Anna trying out her first ballet slippers. They were all around me in the emptiness, and I'd get kind of maudlin and end up turning on the TV and knitting in front of the TV emptiness, which at least had sound.

So when Deal knocked on the door, I was more curious than anything.

"Hello, Jonah," he said.

Lord, I can't remember when he last called me "Jonah." That is my true name, but he'd lately called me "Joanie" or "Mother" or just not used a name at all when he addressed me.

"Hello, Deal," I said. "What's up?"

"Jonah," he said for the second time, "may I come in for a moment?"

"Of course, Deal," I said.

We settled ourselves in the living room. I'd replaced the empty spot left by the red leather chair with a lovely old rocker I picked up at a yard sale. It had a carved design on the top of the back, looked like a twisting branch with leaves, and I'd sanded and sealed it 'til it shone. I'd made electric blue cushions for it that jazzed up the room some since our old blue sofa was so faded. I liked sitting and rocking there. I felt pretty brazen actually 'til I got used to it. After all, this had been Deal's spot for so long. It took a surprising amount of courage to sit there. I kept thinking I should move, but I'd make myself stay 'til I got used to the power that seemed to arise from that spot. I wanted to shy away from that power. After a while, it became a place that let me meditate on my identity, who I'd like to be in the months and years ahead.

I sat in the rocker, and Deal sat on the sofa, kind of hunched forward. I offered Deal some iced tea. He said he wasn't thirsty. "You're looking well," he said.

"Thank you," I said. I thought it was rude to say that he wasn't looking all that well, actually. He was thinner, which might not have been a bad thing, but there was an uncertainty to him I'd never seen before. His skin still had his characteristic dark tint, but it didn't glow like it used to, after a day out on the farm. It looked more like he'd bought some fake tan color at the drugstore and rubbed it on and it didn't quite penetrate.

"Jonah," he said for the third time, "you know I'm not living here, but I'm working here every day. I have to drive for miles after a long day to get to the apartment, and I have to drive for miles before the sun's up to get here. I have to bring a sandwich with me for lunch 'cause I don't dare come in the house." Deal looked around the room as if he were trying to recognize it. "I spent my life doing for all of you. I spent my life keeping this house in our family, and I don't dare come in it any more without your say-so." Deal looked about to cry, and I looked around for a box of Kleenex. Probably it was by my chair in the family room where I had moved the TV, but I didn't dare leave the living room to get it for him. I thought he'd think a Kleenex was an insult to his manliness.

"I hear you're working part-time at the bank," he continued, "and I thought it would make more sense for you to move to a place in town near where you're working. Then I could move back here where I work," he said all in a rush.

"Why, Deal," I said, "of course it would make sense." I kind of emphasized the word *sense*. "But you've often said I don't have good sense, and I don't feel like changing at this late stage in the game."

"But, Jo," he said.

Using the name "Jo" was really hitting below the belt because that had been his pet word for me. "Jo." And I hadn't heard it in such a long darn time, and I was going to need that Kleenex myself if I didn't get him out of there quick.

"Nice of you to drop by, Deal," I said. "Give my best to Dawn." And I rose to let him know that the visit was over, the way my boss did at the bank. The way they do in the movies.

"Now, Jonah…" he started.

But I cut him off. "Don't 'Jonah' me, Deal Strayhorn," I said, and I held up my head like I was passing out money at the bank. "You made your bed, so to speak. Now you'll be lying in it whether you like it or not."

"Could you at least ask the kids if they would consider coming by now and then?" he asked at the threshold as he turned to leave. He spoke in a hoarse whisper, so I almost couldn't hear him.

"Deal," I said, "I can talk to them, but they have minds of their own. I didn't tell them not to visit you, and I doubt they'll listen to me on this subject. Do some reaching out. Get outside that damn chair, why don't you, and start you some kindnesses toward folks. See whether that doesn't get you a mite closer to what you're looking for in this world. There aren't any lions left to tame out here on this prairie, but you have some mighty fine offspring who've been longing for you right and left since they were just so very, very small. And they've plain given up on you, Deal. They've plain given up."

When I heard his truck pull out of the drive, I grabbed the throw I had on the TV sofa, and I grabbed the Kleenex, and then I grabbed a sofa pillow and hugged it to my chest like a baby. I went back in the living room and sat in that damn rocker and rocked my poor heart out until it was the wee hours of the morning. I had to laugh to think that I'd found a way to spend the evening all right without any knitting or TV at all.

DEAL

After two months, I'm still at the apartment—need I say more? I am living in an *apartment*, for God's sake.

I've been sleeping on the couch—when I can sleep. I've lost my talent for sleeping. I get up and pace around the tiny living room at night. Sometimes, I go out on the tinier patio and smoke a cigarette even though I haven't smoked since Vietnam. Dawn may join me. We don't say a whole lot. She's looking for a job in Kansas City, near her mother's. I told her I'd pay for her to finish college, but she's not certain she wants to go. She has big circles under her eyes, all around her eyes really. She looks kind of like a raccoon. I have no idea what I look like. I don't check the mirror very carefully. Scared to face myself, I guess. I do know I'm pulling my belt tighter and tighter. I had to cut the end off it the other day. It was hanging down way too long. Somebody would have noticed I've lost a little weight.

Dawn comes and goes, her moods, that is. Otherwise, she doesn't move. She sits in the red leather chair and naps or paints her toenails. One day, she's affectionate, kind of frolicky. Like a puppy. The next day, she's sour and unavailable. Like an apple picked too soon. The next day, I come home to a siren, all gauzy and with that smell.

This morning, I got up early, like I always do, and tiptoed around the little kitchen holding my work boots in my left hand so I wouldn't clomp around and wake her up. I turned on the tap and put some water in a pot to fix a thermos of iced tea for later. When I went to set the pot on the stove, one of my boots hit the pot, and water spilled all over the floor. Darn. I set the boots down, grabbed some paper towels, and here comes Dawn, flimsy robe open, crotch winking at me below this postage stamp-sized nightgown and screeching. "You insane geriatric. You clumsy son-of-a-bitch."

"Good morning to you too," I said hoping to get out of there fast, maybe buy the tea on the way, trying not to look at her nether parts.

"What am I supposed to do here all day while you're working?" she asked, sullen but not screeching.

"Whatever you do," I said inching backward.

"I don't do anything." Her face got real long. "I fix myself up and sit."

"Well, how about you don't sit in that red leather chair when you're painting your nails. You're gonna' get some of that lacquer on the upholstery where it won't come off."

"It's not lacquer," she said. "It's high gloss polish, and I'm careful."

"We'll talk further tonight," I said, kind of like you do when your kid's put a dent in your pickup. "I've got to check fences this morning. Can't have deer in the corn."

"Deer in the corn," she mimicked me. "Deer in the corn. We can't have deer in the corn." She pulled her robe closed and then flashed me. "No deer in the corn, no honey in the sack," she said.

I threw the wet paper towels in the trash, grabbed my work boots, and high-tailed it out to the truck sock footed. It took me a while to settle down, but the whirring of my pick-up calmed me. I like a piece of machinery that's tuned right.

Every day, driving out to the farm, driving back from the farm too, for that matter, I think about Jonah, my sweet Jo. I think about all the years I never spoke to her that much or hugged her extra. I was doing my living either in one of my tractors or my combine or hiding out in that red chair. Dreaming of being strong, virile, swarthy, a real man. And the funny thing, the totally ironic thing about it all is that I have been a strong man. The strongest. I was a deacon at Maranatha Baptist too, upright, decent, better than just plain strong. I never let my family go hungry. One season the drought was so bad, my best land was eighty bushel corn, and my sandy soil wasn't even worth harvesting. I harvested mostly dust. So I got a job in town at the 7-Eleven at night. Jonah made quilts and sold 'em and made corncob dolls and such and sold 'em, and we pulled through. When people saw me in the 7-11, they knew why I was there. It was no sin. They were harvesting dust too. The crop insurance check helped me keep the farm. The 7-Eleven checks kept us fed.

I went to see Jonah the other day. I was asking to move back in to the house so I could be closer to work, but, really, I just wanted an excuse to see her. She's lost weight too, but she didn't look haggard, not at all. She looked soft and warm and very precious, like my bride. She has this funny round face, like a girl in a movie I saw a long time ago. She's always been my pumpkin—Jo. I wanted to take her in my arms and rock her, but I've never been a great talker, and the words—ah, there were no words. She dismissed me as she should have. She's very proud. She's doing a good job at the bank, I know. She's always done a good job at home. I never knew she had a head for figures, but I knew she had a heart for people. I've been kind of like Anna, our daughter the dancer. I've been so busy dancing, and aimin' high, I couldn't walk on my own ground, the ground that I planted.

Chapter 7

JONAH

Anna is my torment. She is my fourth child. Field, Wally, and Daniel are the three boys. Anna is my only daughter. Field is a contractor, married to Alicia. They have two kids, a girl and a boy. Wally had been married to Dawn, of course. No kids. Such a blessing for everyone as things turned out. Daniel has three boys, very dear. He married an older woman, very solid and fine, Manya, originally from Russia. One of the boys is hers, and two are theirs. Daniel is my intellectual. He teaches history and is finishing up his doctorate at KU. He is so full of love. He was always the best hugger in the family. He instinctively knew just how to be with me, soft or rowdy, to joggle me out of a low spell and get me back to this world. He is a smiler too, always smiling.

But Anna is my torment. Seems like nothing I ever did or said hit that girl quite right. Back when she was still living at home, if I said, "Anna, you're looking really pretty today. I love that scarf," she'd say, "Now, Mother, you don't have to fake it. I know you don't like the way I dress."

If I said, "Anna, why don't you give your hair a brushing before you go out," she'd give me the most hateful look, really stern and glowering, and say, "Can't you ever say anything nice to me, ever?"

She was such a sweet baby and such a funny toddler. She'd crack us up by the cute things she did, like trying to get the dog to race with her toy duck. She had some of those toys that you pull on a stick when you're learning to walk, like a duck whose webbed feet roll along as you pull it. She had one of those lawn mowers that you put bubble liquid into, and the lawn mower would blow bubbles and go clack clack as she pushed it along. She had wavy, thick hair, dark as Deal's, and her brothers and I would gather around and say, "What a good job you're doing, Anna, mowing the lawn."

One day, I guess she was about six or seven, all that changed. She didn't snuggle up to me anymore, just to her daddy. It was like she thought she had to choose up sides to be able to survive in our family. I lost her then, and I didn't know how to get her back. Like I said before, if I reached out, she'd slap me down, and if I didn't, she'd spit.

ANNA

Let me speak! My name is Anna, and I dance.

She just doesn't get it—why Daddy left. He's been bored with her for years. All she ever does is cook and clean and can, and at night, maybe knit or watch TV. Even though she went to two years of college before she got married, she doesn't really read very much. She doesn't seem to care about music or art or dance or theater. Her religion is fixing a hot dish for sick people. She doesn't know theology or philosophy or politics or ANYTHING. She's so ignorant. She doesn't fix herself up except to go to church, and then she wears a dress that she probably got before Field was born. She is DUMPY. She is PALE. Why does SHE have to be my mother?

I have COLOR. She likes to say my colors are so bright they could catch fire. I like my colors. Why should she be criticizing the way I am? She's never gotten me, never. I remember when I was a little girl, I wanted to wear spangled ribbons in my hair. They didn't have all those fancy barrettes back then, but I could envision them before their time. When Mama went shopping, I took my allowance and bought two pink ribbons. I took two of my plain old plastic barrettes, put some glue on them and on the ribbons, and sprinkled glitter on them. When everything dried, I shook it off on a piece of paper, like my teacher did, and slowly poured the excess back into the glitter vial.

I was extremely proud of myself because usually I wasn't quite so careful. I was more impulsive, and of course, sometimes being impulsive, I broke things, and then I got in trouble with Mama. Daddy didn't seem to care.

Anyway, I was so careful that day to do it right, and I was so proud of those glitter ribbon barrettes. I was proud of having COLOR AND DOING IT RIGHT, BOTH. I thought I had fixed my impulsiveness, even though I didn't know that word back then. I thought now, finally, Mother would be proud of me, and would "get" me, and show me off to her friends at church with the beautiful sparklies I had made myself.

First, she complained because even though I'd been so careful, some of the glue had gotten stuck in the rug. Come on, I mean, I was only about eight or something. Then she complained because even though they were mostly dried, some of the glue got stuck in my hair. She was embarrassed because the other little girls didn't wear glitter. I mean, come on, I was ahead of my time. That was the whole point. She didn't know what the teacher would think. Who gave a goddamn fuck what the stupid teacher would think? Actually, I think I liked that teacher, and she probably would have told me how creative I was. Mother said I couldn't wear my beautiful glitter ribbon barrettes to school. She said if I really wanted to, I could wear them around the house. AROUND THE HOUSE? JESUS CHRIST, WHAT'S THE POINT?

So, you can see, we started scrapping when I was young. Deep down, we weren't made out of the same cloth or the same barrette either. When I was older, and I remembered about me making those cute barrettes, you know what I thought? I didn't really think Mother minded so much about the glue. She was clean, sure, but she didn't clean all the time or complain about the house not being perfect. I have to give her that. So I didn't really think it was about the glue in the rug or the glue in my hair. I thought it was about the color, the sparkle. She just couldn't stand to see it for some reason.

Chapter 8

JONAH

It was totally unexpected, some time after Deal left, when Anna called me to see if she could come over and talk. She was waitressing then, supposedly saving money to move to New York to dance, and I'd see her from time to time if I wandered into her café for lunch. She definitely didn't call me to tell me about her life, the way some young girls do with their mothers. Of course, I said, "Sure, come on over," but I was nervous about it.

She looked great when she came in. She liked to wear her hair back, the way dancers do, and wear funny combinations of colors like plum and dark green or orange and lilac. Sometimes, I worried that her colors were so bright they'd burn her. But she was thin and tall and had a darker tinge to her skin, like Deal, and those colors looked so fine on her. She shimmered like a grackle in the sun. I knew she wouldn't believe it, though, if I said anything, so I stuck to "hi" and how good it was to see her and was she hungry or anything.

"Mother," she said, "I'm not going to beat around the bush. I know you don't like me very much. We've never really seen eye to eye, have we?"

I kept quiet and held on because I knew she didn't want to hear me object.

"Mother, what are you going to do with yourself, now that we're all gone? You can't just be hanging around this old place, can you? The chores are pretty much done, aren't they? You don't have any more kids to control or a husband either. So if I were you," she said, "I'd move to town and let Daddy have this place. He has to be over here to work the land, you know, and you don't really need to be here. So why be so selfish? This was his family's homeplace anyway. You owe it to him. Plus, if you hadn't been so involved in our lives, maybe you could have paid a little more attention to him along the way, and he'd still want you around."

I don't know what came over me then. I'd always tried to find a way to placate Anna even though hardly anything had ever worked.

I stood up so fast, my foot hit the coffee table, and it tipped over with her purse and with my little cut glass candy box, and the little square pastel mints went all over the rug and all over her purse. I didn't want to say something or do something I'd be sorry for the rest of my life, and I didn't want to ask her to leave. It was her house too. I felt completely stymied.

"Ooh, I knew I couldn't talk sense to you," she said, shaking her head like I was the kid and she was the frustrated parent. "I'm out of here," she said, and she walked on out to her car.

Devastated. I couldn't catch my breath. One time, when I was in second grade, and I was walking home from school, a boy from my class, Freddy Jay Rickey, came out of nowhere and, for no reason I know of, punched me in the stomach as hard as he could. I screamed, and a lady in a two-story house across the way must have had her window open and heard me. She stuck her head out and yelled, "You, boy, you git now. Get out of here." And he ran away. That was the first time I knew what it meant to have the wind knocked out of you.

After Anna sashayed off, I guess I spent most of the day sitting on the sofa holding my stomach, those little mints still all over the floor. Devastated as I was, I knew she really had no clue that she'd hurt me so bad. She just thought I was her enemy. A block of wood. An unfit mother. As the righteous child, the misunderstood child, she thought she had the higher moral ground. I can remember being the same with my mother. And I bet my mother was the same with her mother. So in a way, I felt I deserved my daughter's treatment. It was payback for generations of immigrant mothers whose hearts could not find the proper language to speak to their daughters in the New World. Although I was Kansas born and bred, I might as well have been as Old World as my mother, Anna, who came from Latvia, because there was clearly an ocean between my daughter, Anna, and myself.

Maybe she was right too about leaving and letting Deal stay in the house. He and Dawn could cozy up in front of the fire instead of wasting this place by sitting like I did holding my stomach in hopes of catching a breath of air that might stir my way. What was it that Dawn had said that day, "It would be a cushy life." Maybe I should move on over and let her have that cushy life. Although, to tell the truth right then, I couldn't imagine moving from the house. At that moment, I couldn't even imagine moving from the sofa.

ANNA

After I saw Mother, I went over to talk to Daddy. Actually, I called him to meet him in town for lunch at this place I work. Honestly, I thought I understood why he'd left, and I was all for him starting a new life that brought him more excitement, well, at least more happiness, than the old, but I wasn't quite ready to see him with a girlfriend just yet.

After he sat down, he thanked me, like three or four times, for inviting him. That was so unlike Daddy. I didn't see why he was doing all this thanking exactly. So we're talking, and I'm telling him about my plans for saving up to go to New York to dance. Anyway, finally, I got around to tellin' him that I understood why he left, and I didn't hold it against him. He lit into me so bad, oh my God.

"What do you understand, Anna?" he asked me in a really fierce tone, which, again, is not like Daddy.

"Whoa, Daddy," I said, "calm down. I'm on your side. I'm just sayin' that Mother is not all that much fun. She's kind of plain, and well she's nice enough to most people, but I can see why you'd want more for yourself."

"Anna," he said real quiet now, "your mother is practically a saint. She's about the best woman there could be in the whole world. She spent her young years raising you kids. If you don't think it's glamorous rinsing out diapers or shucking corn and squashing corn borers, you're right. It's so far from glamorous, it's like another planet." He shook his head so hard and got so red in the face, I thought he might have a stroke. "It's like it's another planet," he said again. "But it was our planet, the planet we chose together. I believe she loved it on this planet with me and with all of you for a long, long time.

"'Twas me was the fool, Anna." He stood up, and I looked around. I was afraid my boss might notice. "'Twas your father that was the fool. So let's hear no more words against your mother—ever."

"But, Daddy," I protested, sputtering. "I've always been on your side, and you've always been on mine. I thought we understood each other. I thought you wanted me to be against Mother. You were all the time telling her she didn't have good sense. I only wanted to be on the side that did have good sense, on your side."

He almost started crying then. I could see his eyes well up. Here I was nearly twenty-four, and I don't believe I'd ever seen my daddy cry. It was startling. He rubbed the side of his eye, like people do who are pretending a gnat is bothering them instead of owning up and bawling. I felt like my whole picture of the universe was wrong, like all the stances I'd taken in my family my whole life had been called into question, and I didn't know who I was any more if I wasn't his ally.

Chapter 9

WALLY

Sometimes, people in a large family get lost. They say a middle child gets lost in a family of three. I was the middle child of the first three boys.

Field was the athlete, and Daniel was the student. I was just somebody in between that Deal didn't really bother to know. Then came Anna. She blurted herself out wherever she was. Dressed like a gypsy. Couldn't miss her.

My claim to fame was actually two things: money and a beautiful wife and maybe shoving Deal's ignorance of me up his ass by working for Sutter's, a company he'd always hated. I don't know exactly why he hated them. Gave him a raw deal on the price of corn once, I guess. He has a long memory. As do I. As do I.

After I tried to kill him, I got off on probation because I'd been such a model white Christian, but, hey, this is a small town, and everybody knew about it. It's a town where you don't ever get off of anything. Not for a minute.

So my boss called me in. "Hey there, Wally, sit down why don't you, son. I hear you've been on a rampage. That right?"

"Cut the 'son' crap, Brad," I said. "You firing me or not?" Odd how these words poured out when Brad and I had been getting along for five years with few feathers ruffled. He generally bossed from afar, knowing he could rely on me to follow the guidelines and the deadlines. Occasionally, a pat on the back or a minor caution. We had a regular golf game too with some of the guys.

"Whoa, Wally," he said. "Don't take it out on me. I know it's rough times."

"Sorry, Brad." I said, "Are you firing me or what?"

"Got to let you go," he said. "Can't have trigger happy folks on the payroll. Bad PR for the company. Sorry, Wal. You're a good employee too. And a fairly good golf partner."

"I'm out of here," I said and packed up.

Beautiful wife gone; money gone; golf gone; shoving it up Deal's bony ass gone. Whew.

ANNA

One fine day, Wally invited me to go canoeing with him. I was so totally hyper, wanting to get out of my routine: workouts, waitress, workouts, research dance schools on the Internet, workouts, etc., that I bobbed around my apartment getting ready. Especially, after both Mother and Daddy were, to put it mildly, unwelcoming. I might be an orphan, but at least I had a brother that wanted to hang with me. So what if I was a little scared. Who wouldn't be? I'd never been canoeing before.

It was a Saturday, and I didn't have to go to work 'til late. Hallelujah.

Wally said to bring a water bottle and some sunscreen and a waterproof jacket if I had one. He said he'd take me on an easy river, but take a change of clothes, just in case. I could just picture me falling into this creek…river, whatever. Oh my God. We needed two cars to run the shuttle. I didn't know exactly what he meant, but whatever.

I put my hair up in a baseball cap, a red one, and grabbed my aquamarine rain jacket. I'd picked it up at a thrift store and hadn't worn it yet, so I didn't really know how waterproof it might be. With my favorite glamour-puss sunglasses, I was ready to roll.

Wally was right on time as always. I had The White Stripes clashing away on my CD player, and I'd brought some granola bars for later. Wally said he'd bring the lunch. The canoe was on top of his car. Easy to follow.

We took the back roads. They're marked "scenic" on the map, and most definitely, some days, in good old mostly flat Kansas, you feel this incredible spiritual power. It must be a vortex or something. Other days, though, it'll drive you crazy living here, it's so desolate. That's one reason I want to move to New York. You're not going to look out your apartment window in Brooklyn and see miles upon miles of grassland or old homesteads that haven't been repainted since before I was born. Plus, in Kansas, there are no diagonals, not on the back roads anyway. The land is divided up into what they call "sections." They're all rectangles. The roads run north and south or east and west. Some of the highways run diagonally, but we weren't on a highway. I'm hoping in New York they believe in diagonals. Truly, diagonals are not that novel, but they can really change your point of view.

We were driving through what's called the Flint Hills. There's just enough dirt covering the flint rock underneath to grow bluestem grass for cattle to feed on. Everybody you talk to out here, they'll tell you, "It's the richest grassland anywhere." They're so proud of it. Makes you wonder, okay, if the grass is so rich, why are people not more prosperous?

We drove through the Tallgrass Prairie National Preserve. Plenty of grass there, but how ironic can you get that they have to create a preserve not to lose the prairie. I mean, come on, the prairie. That's the good old US of A personified. Our pioneer spirit and all that.

After about an hour and a half, we got to a spot by a bridge where there were some cars parked. "Park yours, here, Anna," Wally said. "This is the take-out."

I put my stuff in Wally's car and locked mine.

"The pioneers traveling west on the Oregon Trail crossed this very creek," Wally said as we started up in his car. He was wearing a jacket for paddling. I would bet it was definitely waterproof. I don't think he picked it up locally.

"In fact, later," Wally said, "I can show you the cemetery where quite a few of those pioneers are buried. We can walk in the ruts their wagon trains made one hundred and fifty years ago. Isn't that amazing? And you never know. We might see an eagle while we're out on the river. Keep your eyes peeled."

"Hmm," I think I said. I was starting to freak about actually getting into a boat. The wind had come up too. It does that out here. You go out on a nice warm day, and pretty soon the wind'll have you wondering whether you should change your plans.

At the place he called the "put-in," we unloaded the canoe, paddles, and life vests, and he tied in a special bag that kept the food and small items dry. The canoe was really heavy, but we didn't have to carry it too far.

"You ready for this, kid?" Wally asked.

"Sure," I said clenching my paddle. "No problem."

I was to be in front and look out for rocks that Wally couldn't see. He was the one to steer, but I was the power, he said. He showed me a few canoe strokes before we left the bank.

"We should have some good water from yesterday's rain," he said looking upstream. "But don't worry, Anna. There are only a few rapids of any consequence on this river, and I've never had any problem. If there are people ahead of us, wait 'til they've passed through. If we do tip, float on your back with your feet pointed downstream 'til you find a place to get out.

"No matter what, hold on to your paddle, and whatever you do, don't grab the gunnels. That makes the boat unsteady."

I wasn't really clear what gunnels were, but in the newness of everything, I forgot to ask.

We did really well floating along. We didn't talk much, just paddled and looked at the scenery. There were huge trees framing the shore and occasionally a clear spot where farmland edged down to the riverbank. Very rustic and calming.

Close to lunchtime, I got up the nerve to ask him if he missed Dawn. I should have kept my mouth shut and not spoiled the tranquility.

"Not really," he said.

That should have been enough for me, but no, I had to go on.

"Well, do you miss Dad?"

"Yes," he said.

"Did you really try to shoot him?" I was glad I was up in front. I don't think he could see how scrunched up my face was, dreading his answer.

"I'm not sure," he said. "I was pretty drunk. Soon as the police tackled me, I passed out."

Once again, that should have been more than enough. But I kept on.

"It's a shame for all of us," I said, "that Mother couldn't hold on to her man. If only she could have kept herself a little more up to date."

Wally smacked the water with his paddle. Sounded like a shot. I lurched sideways, grabbed what turned out to be the gunnels, and dropped my paddle. The boat tipped and overturned. Somehow, I found myself with the boat upside down over me, and the boat and I were rushing down the river. I tried to lie on my back and go feet first like he'd told me, but mainly I was trying to get out from under the boat. I got turned around, and my back and legs got slammed sideways against a wide shelf of rock. The boat had flipped onto its side so that the bottom of the canoe smashed me flat against the rock, and the open part of the canoe began to fill with water.

At first, I panicked and wore myself out trying to push the canoe off me with my hands, but it didn't begin to budge. Then I realized I could breathe fine, and I tried to stay calm and think. I managed to get myself turned so my legs went down into the water, but the boat continued to fill. The water was very cold, bracing at first, and then freezing my legs, my arms, and my body. The boat kept filling and pressing against the rock and against my chest and shoulders. I thought, come on; at any minute, Wally will get his footing and rescue me. Meanwhile, I was pinned and growing number by the second.

A powerful memory of being a little girl and nestling into the crook of my mama's arm visited me. My mama was wearing this ugly green apron she had when I was a kid, with little red barns on it with silos. It was so ugly, but I loved that apron. It was my mama to me back then. I remembered her holding me close with that apron on, I must have skinned my knee or something and come in to show her while she was cooking. Mama was humming to me and comforting me. She had her special rosy Mama smell, and she was all lit up like a star.

With renewed drive, I tried again to work myself out from behind the boat. I scraped my left shoulder against the rock to move my shoulder like an inch. Then I worked my right shoulder over an inch. It felt like I was rubbing a layer of skin off my back each time I moved. The boat was so heavy against me with all that rushing water pouring into the front side of it, I felt like it was going to crush my sternum. I treaded water for momentum. My legs were strong but not strong enough to wriggle me loose.

Here's the weirdest part. My mama, shining in her silo apron, jumped in the river with me. She climbed up on the flat shelf of rock in some old tennis shoes and sat down at the edge. With legs bent, she pressed her feet firmly against the back of the boat and heaved with all her might. A space, wide as a finger, opened between me and the boat. Just enough for me to slip free.

All of a sudden, I was being whooshed downstream. I remembered to lie on my back with my feet up. I barely had strength left to steer myself toward shore. Somehow, I maneuvered around rocks and edged toward land. Finally, I dragged myself onto the bank and lay there shivering. It seemed like forever 'til Wally sat beside me, rubbing the parts of me that were not scraped raw, trying to get me warm. He kept saying, "Damn," and banging his fist against the ground and saying, "Oh, Anna, damn. Are you okay, Anna? You gonna' be okay?"

Wally yelled to some folks canoeing upstream, and they ferried a log from the bank to pry our boat away from the rock shelf. Using the rope tied to the front of the boat, they steered it over to us and dumped all the water out. “Thanks a lot,” Wally told them.

“No problem, man,” they said. “Is she all right?”

I tried to examine my injuries, but most of them were on my back. I gingerly walked around to determine whether I would ever dance again. “I’m fine,” I said with bravado. “Thanks for rescuing our boat.”

“Sorry, we couldn’t get up to you sooner,” they said.

Wally still had his paddle, but mine appeared to have floated on down without me as had my VIP sunglasses. I didn’t ever want to step foot back in that boat, but there wasn’t any other way to get to the car. Wally promised we’d paddle as close to the shore as possible, and I eased myself into the canoe with my eyes closed and body trembling while he held it steady. We drifted a little ways to a sunny spot so I could really warm up, and we nibbled our lunch.

“Boy, Anna, you almost bought it back there,” Wally said.

What a comfort a brother can be. I wish I had brought a flask, not just granola bars.

The rest of the way back, Wally did all the paddling. He kept saying, "I’m sorry, Anna. This river is really easy, no kidding.”

I didn’t say much. What could I say? “Gee thanks, you almost got me killed.”

From then on, I bet I saw every scrap of weed, every dragonfly, every damn rock on that stupid river, keeping my arms locked so as not ever again to grab the gunnels—those are the top edges of the boat—by mistake. We never did go to the cemetery where the pioneers are buried. We never did walk in the ruts their wagons made one hundred and fifty years ago, and we never saw a damn eagle. I was just glad I had a change of clothes in the car.

I called my boss to see if he could find a replacement for me for tonight. "Just this once," I said. "I'm all scraped up. My stupid brother nearly got me killed in a canoe." I must have sounded kind of whiny. I hate a whiner. On the other hand, I think I'll get the night off. He said he'd call me back.

Chapter 10

JONAH

I woke up this morning feeling so angry. I wanted to do some damage. I wanted to claw the eyes out of a cat. I wanted to destroy every object in my living room. I wanted to hurl things and rip things, shred things.

All these weeks I've been good old Mom, small town girl. Placid. Lake Placid—where they hosted the Winter Olympics. Well, the Flint Hills are now hosting the sexual Olympics. Come one. Come all. And me, I've been standing on the sidelines as the torch is passed down First Street, saying, "Oh, go right ahead, dear, and destroy our lives. I don't care. I'm just your wifie-poo, your little dustbin. Do with us as you will.

"Take your son and shake his brains out. I'll stand by and watch. Never a whimper out of me. I'm your helpmeet in our destruction. Is there anything else you'd like to take with you? Need a spatula for your new kitchen?"

The more I think about it, the more I want to cause real havoc somewhere. Not just stew. The stew has stewed long enough. It is boiling. The lid is thumping. I wish I were milk in a pot. When I overflowed, I'd be so pretty, spewing a white geyser all over the stove. Sticky stuff to clean up afterward. That's all. Just like Deal, spewing his geyser.

The thought makes me double over and want to vomit. My husband messing with that girl. That girl that was Wally's wife.

Oh, poor Wally. The fire went out from under me completely. All that oomph I had a second ago, drained out. I was bowed down, bowled over with his misery. My son, Wally. Poor Wally.

ANNA

Doing leg exercises at the barre in a studio in Kansas City, where I took class several times a week, I tried not to remember that wild and wooly canoe trip. At night, I'd put Beyoncé or Usher on my headphones really loud to fall asleep, but sometimes, I'd gulp awake, drinking in air, trying not to drown 'til I turned on the bedroom light. I suppose the memory continued to bug me because those moments in the water had truly felt like a brush with death. Not to be dramatic, but I do think that death was playing with me there, trapped behind the canoe with the cold water endlessly flowing.

And the image of my mama, with her ugly red and green Mama apron with the goddamn silos, hugging me and shining like a star was on the fringe of my mind like an, oh God, here I go, like an angel watching over me when I was in danger. I wasn't fighting her, I wasn't yelling at her, I wasn't "educating" her. She was my solace and my light. My mama.

So the glowy kind of feeling I got, remembering the light, kind of played havoc with the family history in my mind. Maybe there'd been a time when I had called her "Mama" not "Mother," and we were close. Maybe there was a chance that the history I'd been taking for granted as long as I could remember was a revisionist history. If Mama and I had had a relationship earlier on that was loving and trusting, my whole picture of our current family entanglements and estrangements would have to be revisited and maybe revised again in the light of, well…light. Re-revising family history was too overwhelming to deal with, so mostly I didn't. But the possibility lingered, like the light, on the edge of my consciousness.

Chapter 11

JONAH

After Deal left, the kids stopped speaking to him one by one. First, of course, was Wally, but the others soon followed.

Despite their misgivings, a few months after Deal left, Field and his wife, Alicia, and their two kids accepted an invitation to Deal & Dawn's for dinner. D & D's. I think of it that way, kind of like a diner or corner grocery or bait shop or something. D & D's turned out to be a small apartment, like a starter home for young marrieds in a complex near the college. Not anywhere near as sweet as the home Wally had bought for Dawn. Course, Dawn didn't know the financial score when she took up with Deal. That red leather armchair had been mighty seductive was my guess, and not just a little misleading.

Field had taken to coming over to check on me a couple of times a week after work, once I filled him in on the situation, and he told me about their visit.

"Mom," he said, "I saw Deal's chair first thing when we walked into the new living room. It stood out like a sunburned nose between a black-and-white plaid sofa and black-and-white plaid recliner. Where'd they get that stuff? Goodwill?"

"The red leather chair?" I asked a little hesitantly. "Just how was it situated?"

"Situated? What do you mean? It was facing the TV."

So it faced the TV. My guess was Deal had taken to hiding out in it again. Funny, how just three months after he left, I could picture D & D's domestic life without my organs wanting to lurch out of my body. At the bank, I smiled at people I'd known all my life, and I didn't even think to bow my head. God knows why. I cannot explain it. Instead of feeling as washed out as the old bills we retired from circulation, I felt as bountiful as the million dollars I was handing out every day. Unless, of course, I wandered into the Mom corners of my mind where I worried about my children or ached for them. Wally especially.

I fixed Field a beer and some nachos, and he continued.

"Everyone was very polite, Mom. Dad grilled the kids some burgers out on their little patio. It was about eight square feet. Dawn put out some chips and had some store-bought cookies for dessert. It was very nice of them to have us over, but I don't get the whole thing. It doesn't make any sense. Is this like a mid-life crisis or what?"

"I don't know, son." I pulled some knitting out of the basket on the chair next to me.

"The kids were on their best behavior," Field continued, "but after we got home and put them to bed, Alicia started sobbing and, goddamn it, she cried for hours. One minute, she was clutching me tight as a vise, and the next minute, she was pounding me with her fists and hollering with all her strength, but in a whisper so she wouldn't wake the kids, 'That bastard. That f-ing son of a bitch. That whore.'" Field shook his head back and forth so fast, and raised his shoulders up to his ears. Seemed like he was trying to stop hearing Allie cry.

"I don't see how we can go back there. I can barely stand it, seeing Dad with Wally's wife, but Alicia can't stand it at all. I guess it makes her go nuts to see that people can simply up and disappear from your life from one day to the next. She said this sad thing, 'Don't they care if they leave your heart behind?'"

"I could talk to her, Field. Let her know I'm okay."

"I don't know, Mom. I think it's more about her remembering her own childhood. All that crazy family stuff she went through. It's like all those childhood scenes are compressed in her mind. Remember those toys we had sometimes when we were kids? Those little novelty toys? The spongy ones with shapes like flowers or dinosaurs or whatever with no water in them? Then when you put the toy into water, it swells up more and more and more. Until it's a monster. I think Deal's leaving has swelled up Alicia's childhood again." He set his beer down.

"This is a funny thing to say, Mom," he said, "but I'm glad I'm coming out here more. I really like spending time with you. Deal's done us that favor at least."

"I really like spending time with you too, son. The Lord works in mysterious ways."

ALICIA

Calamity. Catastrophe. I thought I was a low-key person, and now, at this late date of age twenty-eight, I find I'm a high-key person. Field will just have to deal with me the way I am. Deal. God, I don't even want that word in my vocabulary. Here's a man, salt of the earth, and his wife, saltess of the earth. They've been like my real parents since Field and I started dating in high school. She, well, really both Jonah and Deal, welcomed me into their family when Field brought me home to introduce me the week before the prom. Jonah even slipped me some money to help me buy my prom dress. She knew I was working after school every day. My own parents were basically nonexistent, but I'm not going into all that right now.

It sure was a pretty prom dress. Field said I looked like a puff of heaven, all pink and floaty. I had silk spike heels dyed pink, and a silk clutch purse dyed pink too. My earrings dripped pearls although they weren't real. It was before everyone had to wear black to the prom to be sophisticated and look like they were going to a funeral. I wasn't normally a pink person. I ran track, after all. I think Field was a little surprised that I could transform myself.

Now I've transformed myself again. I've started cursing (but not in front of the kids, God knows) since *that man* left. Suffice it to say, I'm f-ing mad. I'm not letting some ridiculous mid-life shit stop my kids from having a true extended family with loving parents *and* grandparents. I will not let life get carried away with itself. I will find a way to get Deal and Jonah together again, so help me God.

Chapter 12

JONAH

The house I live in is the house where Deal was born and raised. You can't see the house from the road in summer. Trees line the driveway and have actually grown up into some woods on one side of the house. Deer thrive there and can mess with my garden like the rabbits and gophers do. Eternal vigilance is the price of a few carrots and a lettuce patch. Also, a good chicken wire fence helps and some pie pans flapping in the breeze.

The original farm belonged to Deal's family. He added to the land over the years. *We* added to it over the years. I married into this old house and land, but I raised my children here, so it's got to be partly mine. It's got my heart in it. You can tell I feel guilty that Deal isn't living here too. Damn. It's his own damn fault. Damn. He belongs here. But so do I.

The house was not in good repair when I moved in. Deal had been in Vietnam, and his parents had not been the home repair type. I don't think a lot of people back then were the home repair type. We didn't have those big box stores down the street. More than that, we didn't have the funds or the extra time to worry about loose boards or doors that let cold air in around the edges. Look near downtown, and, more often than not, you will see that there are still a lot of non-home-repair types living here. Many of the houses have not seen a coat of paint in a generation of winters.

Deal never had that easy-going attitude. He was a home repair type from the git-go. He came back from Vietnam with his demons, but they just seemed to help him work extra. If he couldn't sleep, he could fix a drippy faucet. If he had a nightmare, he could make sure all the lights worked. When he first came back, he stripped the shreds of remaining paint off the outside of this place, plank by plank, so the boards were smooth. He repainted it a gleaming white, and he's kept it that way ever since.

I did the curtains. Curtains in every room. No drapes, 'cause mostly the rooms are fairly small and have small windows. Some have the original wavy panes in them. Can't see out of them all that well, but they're antiques, and they fit the mood of the place.

Where I sit, mostly in the living room, the curtains are ivory lace, and they billow out in a breeze. They were the one filmy item in a home of cuts and scrapes. With the red leather chair gone, and the family gone, the curtains take me off billowing with them. I don't have to come back to earth with a jolt to apply first-aid cream and Band-Aids to someone's skinned knee.

Somehow, I will have to make peace with the house that betrayed me. A house of floorboards worn and bowed. A house of debts mostly paid. A house of silliness and competence. A house of mistakes. A house of extra canning, just in case. A house of homework and pies set to cool. A house once of love.

There is no cat just now to come and sit in my lap. There is no dog begging for supper. Somehow, when the kids grew up, we let the last pet lapse and didn't renew. Maybe I should check the pound. A house with just me in it doesn't have enough legs scratching fleas while the tail thumps. It's way too quiet although the birds rejoice at the feeders and the mice babies multiply.

I was always complaining about the size of the rooms. When the six of us were running around, we were right on top of each other. Deal built the sun porch for me to get some space. But now that it's just me, I want to sit in a smaller area most of the time so I feel surrounded. The walls take care of me. Funny, isn't it? What used to hem me in comforts me now.

Old stuff everywhere. Vintage is supposed to mean quality. Hah. Maybe in wine. Maybe in cars. Maybe in men. With women, like me, left to our own devices, vintage means spinster or widow or dumped for a secretary.

It's time to refresh. Spruce up. But at the moment, I just want to sit down. Ploomph go the sofa cushions as I take a load off. The frayed strands on the rim of that cushion need to be tucked in and resewn, but betrayal is tiring.

When I get my energy back, refresh I shall. Lots of spruce. He will not recognize me on the street. He'll tip his hat (John Deere cap, more like) before he realizes it's me. I'll nod slightly and walk on. Head held high. Fantasy, thy name is woman. Forget it, I just don't have the energy. I don't keep the garden up the way I used to, and I close off some of the upstairs rooms in the winter. No use to heat everything up there any more. I never *want* to close anything off though. What if one of the kids were to come back home for a while? I'd want to have their room ready, the bed made up fresh, and a vase with flowers standing by. Their ghosts are living there all the time anyway. I don't want to freeze them out.

Chapter 13

ALICIA

One day, while the kids were at school, I finally got up the nerve to call Anna to see if she could come over before her shift started. I'd been mulling strategy for a while on how to get Deal and Jonah back together, and I thought that two heads might be better than one. I wasn't sure Anna had the motivation to act as my co-conspirator, but there wasn't anyone else.

Field used up all his energy building houses. He was basically passive in family matters, preferring not to get emotional, not to get involved.

Wally, you can forget it. He had written Deal off. Sometimes, we had Wally to dinner. The kids were starting to get comfortable with him, and he really tried to play with them. But I noticed I cut my steak into really small pieces when he was over, I was being so careful not to bring up sensitive topics, like family. Wally was bristly as a porcupine. He would have enjoyed shooting quills into Deal, not helping Deal and Jonah reunite.

Daniel was busy too, teaching, working on his doctorate, a wife and three kids. Plus, he lived in Lawrence.

Anna had some hard edges, but where else could I turn? So I called Anna.

"Look, Anna," I said, as we seated ourselves at the dining room table and I poured us each a glass of Chardonnay, "did you ever see the *Parent Trap* with Hayley Mills? I think they did a remake a few years ago."

"Yeah, I think so," Anna said. Her hair was up in that messy, casual style that's so popular. She seemed captivated by the wine she kept swirling in her glass.

"Well, it's about twins whose parents split up. The twins conspire to get their parents back together. I was wondering…I thought maybe you and I could try getting your parents back together."

"You're kidding, Alicia. My parents? I don't know. I just try not to go there. It's a rotten mess."

"Come on, Anna. We could dream up a few little schemes. My kids need one solid family. And Manya's kids do too. Their Russian family is too far—"

"—Alicia, I don't do heavy emotional lifting," she interrupted and took a sip of her wine. "I mean, what the fuck is wrong with my daddy, carrying on like a teenager? And poor Wally. For Christ's sake, his own son." She took another sip. Then her face brightened. "But the conniving part… I like the conniving part. What ya' got?"

"Well, first, we have to get rid of Dawn."

"Hmm," Anna said, probably thinking of Wally's assault on Dawn's VW bug, "I don't guess we'd better disable her car if we want her to leave."

"No," I agreed.

"Ditto for hurting her in any way. Then she'd just be more alluringly pitiful and couldn't leave as easily."

"Plus, Anna, I know you couldn't hurt her…physically." I wondered if I really did know that about Anna. "So we have to somehow harass her enough, make her life with Deal miserable enough that she'll just figure it's not worth it to stick around, right?"

"Right!"

"We could send her poison pen letters," I said. "We could threaten. Let's see, we could threaten to hurt Deal if she didn't leave."

"Would she even give a flying fuck?" Anna tossed back the sip of wine left in her glass. "Little Miss Beauty Queen. Miss Blond Vamp of the Century. Hey, we could sneak in there one night and cut off her shining locks?"

"Right," I said. "Like we could really sneak in there."

"I know," Anna said, pouring us another round. "Instead of trying to force her out," why don't we set up a lure? What appeals to a vacuous blond bombshell more than a vacuous blond stud? Some Nordic type, maybe. With an accent. Hmm, no, she likes Deal, she likes them tanned, hmm. There's this slightly older, suave guy, younger than Deal, I think he's from Spain. He comes into our café a lot. He's a flirt. I could go over to see Dawn and pretend like, Gee, I guess it's time for us to be friends and invite her over to the café. I could ask him if he'd do me a favor and come on to her. How about that?"

"What if he won't?" I asked and then added, "What if he will, and she doesn't take the bait?"

"I guess we'd have to figure out Plan B," Anna said. "But, hey, Ally." She flashed me a wicked grin. "I didn't have you pegged as so…undercover. This actually sounds entertaining. I think I'm going to have to brush up on my Español."

That night, I put the kids to bed and was looking at the paper for a second before I folded a load of clothes when Anna called. Field had gone back to town for a meeting.

"Can you talk, Alicia?" she asked.

"Yeah," I said.

"It's Plan B already," she said. "I called after I got off work and asked Deal if I could speak to Dawn. Guess what? Dawn has moved the fuck out."

DAWN

I can't say Deal ever mistreated me. He was a gentleman. He never came on too strong or yelled at me. He never called me names or tried to blame me for coming between him and Jonah. He tried to help me figure out what to do next. He offered to pay for me to go back to school.

Yet he disgusted me. His dark, wavy hair never seemed exactly clean. It was always a little greasy like Indians' hair. I know that makes me sound racist, but haven't you noticed whether it's people from India or American Indians, they should have this absolutely gorgeous black, shiny hair, but it's almost always a little greasy.

Deal's hair was like that. Plus, he had black hairs on his thick fingers. And his hands were callused and rough. I gave a little shiver every time I thought about them. Funny, when I was with Wally, I used to fantasize about Deal because he was so…male. My honey would start flowing when I was around him because he had those hormone things, like male insects put out to attract a female. When he came into the house from being out on one of those ginormous farm machines, it was like I was waiting in line to see a movie star. So, you know, when I was with Wally, in bed I mean, I'd sometimes pretend he was Deal.

And then, bam, I was with Deal, and I wanted to get the fuck out of there as fast as I could.

It was kind of like that with the first boy I went with. He looked like a football player. We were in fifth grade, and he had been put back twice, so he had already hit a growth spurt and a puberty spurt. All right, he had a few zits, but he was built. The teacher assigned us seats in that class, so I was sitting by this guy, Joe Hickinson, for weeks just moaning and drooling inside. Finally, I whispered to this girl, Beth Ann, out on the playground that I had a crush on Joe Hickinson. And, of course, she told him, and one day he asked me if I wanted to go steady, and I said, "Okay," and he gave me this big bulky chain to wear around my neck that had a school ring on it. I don't know whose ring it was. It couldn't have been Joe Hickinson's since he was still in fifth grade. But the minute I tried to put that necklace on, I felt sick to my stomach, and I couldn't wear it, and the next day I had to pass him a note to meet me on the playground again, and I had to give the necklace back. Oh my God, what a relief that was, giving that thing back. It was soooo disgusting, even just holding it and thinking about putting it on.

He got back at me by putting me down to some of the other kids when I could overhear. I came in from the playground the next day, all sweaty from jump rope, and my hair had grown pretty long by that point. It was tangled, and I didn't have time to comb it out before the bell rang, and he was whispering to some boys near him and trying to hide the fact that he was pointing at me. I heard the word *dog*, but I didn't care at all, even though I usually would have died a thousand deaths, because I was free of Joe Hickinson and his nasty zits, even though I still had to sit right next to him for the rest of the school year.

I hadn't thought of Joe Hickinson in God knows how long, but it was just like that, the minute I wheeled my luggage into the apartment Deal had rented. I wanted to wheel it right back out, but I had nowhere else to go, so I didn't.

I should have put my pride in my pocketbook and slunk back home to my mom's. But, as nauseous and revolted as I was, I just stayed like a stray cat that's too dehydrated to travel.

The weeks dragged on and on. Deal and I didn't speak that much, but I have to say Deal was always courteous. Once we had his older son and his wife and kids to dinner, sort of implying we were a couple, I guess. Otherwise, I just kind of laid around the apartment trying to think up places to go and things to do. Deal brought food home, and I would fix myself a sandwich or some cereal now and then. I did always keep my hair combed nice, but I didn't even paint my toenails that often.

Then one day, I went out to get some feminine products. I had my period, and I realized that I could still drive just fine. While Deal was at work, I packed up my car and left him a note. It said, "Thanks for being a gentleman." And I was gone.

Chapter 14

DEAL

After Dawn left, at least I could breathe again. I went out on that little brick patio we had and burned the satin sheets she'd been sleeping on. I'm embarrassed to say I'd bought them with a Playboy setup in mind right before Dawn moved in. After she left, I went back to the store and got plain cotton.

Finally, I could sleep in this crummy bed and get off the sofa, but I still wasn't sleeping well, a little better maybe. I'd drag myself out of bed in the morning, fix myself a cup of coffee, a little breakfast, and a lunch pail, and take off for the farm. I'd do whatever needed doing depending on the season or the weather. I could just barely get myself to mend the equipment that was essential but broken. When I got home, I'd get cleaned up, heat up some frozen dinner, maybe have a beer and watch TV. It was not a fun time. I was not feeling funny.

One night, I came in all dirty, exhausted. I'd been dealing with a cranky baler off and on all day. I just couldn't get the tension on the twine calibrated right. It kept getting too loose or too tight, so it broke and hay got stuck in the belly of the baler. My hired hand was as frustrated as I was. We couldn't get a rhythm going. I said, "Rats!" so many times my throat got hoarse.

I got home, and first thing in the door, I saw that red leather chair facing me. It looked so darn surly, arrogant. It stared me in the face, daring me to aspire to some idiotic notion of myself. For God's sake, if I'd really wanted to be a lion tamer, I would have trained to be one years ago. It wasn't ever a genuine aspiration of mine. It was just the notion of...of contending well with savagery. And here I was the one who'd become the savage. And I wasn't contending well with that at all.

Before I could really think, I hit that damn chair with my lunch pail, which, of course, did nothing but scuff up the chair, break the catch on the lunch pail, and dump my foil wrap and dirty napkins across the floor. I was so mad I opened the long blade in my pocketknife. I stared back at that stupid chair for a minute, then I stabbed the chair in the heart. I withdrew the knife, looked at it, and sliced long, deep lines down the seatback and onto the seat. Kind of like I was a butcher, I carved that insolent red leather chair into strips of bloodied meat.

Afterward, I washed the knife and took a shower myself. Then I went out to a bar and got solid drunk.

The next morning, there was cotton in my head and mouth and alfalfa weevils in my stomach. It was still dark out. I turned on the light in the living room and saw the chair. Even though the leather was all shredded, the chair seemed like it was laughing at me. I threw some shorts on, and when I wrestled it out the front door, something clinked on the walk. I smashed the chair into the pickup and drove to the dump. I backed the pickup into the area where people left mangled lawn chairs and rotting refrigerators. I picked up the remains of the red leather chair and hurled them overboard. I gunned the engine out of there and drove on back to the apartment. I felt sick to my stomach and couldn't wait to go back to bed. As I approached the front door, a glint on the walk caught my eye, and I bent down to look. Lying there was a silver pin. I picked it up, but my head was too fuzzy to puzzle over it much. I set it on the first surface I came to, took a couple aspirin, and went back to bed.

When I woke up, I felt better at first, but in the living room was a dead zone where the chair used to be. Like the fields in Vietnam we'd napalmed. Not much left standing.

Jo had suggested I get out of the chair. That wouldn't be a problem now. I chuckled. At least, I could still chuckle. She'd also told me to reach out to my children and grandchildren. That would be one hell of a challenge, given that they pretty much hated me.

But the morning after, as it was, I had an inkling of two places I wanted to start. I wanted to read books—non-fiction books, maybe even fiction books—about farmers, Kansas farmers. Kansas farmers and Kansas dirt. I wanted to know the names of things I'd taken for granted all my life. I figured if the Eskimos had a hundred names for snow, I could look for, maybe, fifty names for dirt. Daniel could tell me where to look. Maybe I'd find the name Deal in there somewhere too. And I wanted to summon up the fortitude to call Pastor Runkle and see how I could redeem my standing at church.

The church had been like a second family to me. Our kids had grown up in Sunday School, church suppers, Christmas festivals, the whole nine yards. In fact, Anna got her first starring role as Mary in a Christmas pageant when she was seven or eight. She might have been the first ever dancing Mary, swinging her doll, the baby Jesus, around the stage.

And I had been exceedingly proud, maybe sinfully proud, of my role as deacon, joining some of the better educated, professional men from town in making decisions about the direction of the church. I'd been elected to represent our congregation, and I thought I'd reflected pretty well the concerns and aspirations of most of our members. After all, I felt that they, like me, had sprung forth from the land that nurtured them and were part and parcel of it.

After leaving Jonah, I had called Pastor Runkle, the minister of Maranatha Baptist, and said I wasn't feeling well and would need to pare down my attendance and my efforts as a deacon. That, plus leaving my home and having most of my children incommunicado, created a desolation in me, the likes of which I never could have imagined, being one who thought he had little need for people.

I reached Pastor Runkle on the first ring.

"Brother Deal," he said. "We've missed you."

I'm not certain what I expected him to say, but his kindness touched me.

"Thanks, Randy," I said. "I've been missing all of you too. I'd like to pay you a visit if you can spare the time."

"Of course, Deal," he said. "Come on in. You just let me know when."

DANIEL

When Deal called, I was in the Do Not Disturb corner of our bedroom where stray parts of my dissertation-in-progress resided. My dissertation was on the history—including the psychological and economic impact—of prairie fires in Kansas farm communities in the twentieth century.

I know I was distracted by the long day: work, the kids, cleaning up from dinner, looking at the piles of books and articles still to be read, but I tried to clear my mind to talk to Deal when he called.

I must say after Manya's initial visit to Mom's, we let our own lives keep us from dealing with Mom and Dad much. Sometimes, Manya took the kids down to see Mom on the weekend so I could get a little more done on the dissertation. Sometimes, I went with them. Mom looked really good. She had more color in her face, and she'd lost a little of her extra weight. She had more "zip" as Manya would say. She always had some new little toys for the kids and loved to bake them cookies. She'd have the cookies ready on the sheet when we arrived, and they could decorate them before she put them in the oven. They loved going to the farm and being with their babushka.

"Daniel," he said when he called. "This is Dad."

Well, of course, I knew who it was the minute he said my name.

Where do emotions come from? They flow into your being like a swirl on a weather map, like a Category 5 hurricane, pictured in all different colors on the TV screen. The swirl makes it hard to think. Do I want to sound distant with this man whom I used to revere as my father, or do I want to be pleasant? I wish he'd just ask to take me fishing one weekend, but, of course, neither of us fish. Just the two of us together, off in a wilderness somewhere, mending.

Maybe I was colder than I intended. I just couldn't get the right voice to come out of that swirl.

"What's up, Deal?" I realized I'd said Deal and not Dad and wished my voice had come up with Dad.

"Daniel, how are you? How's everyone?"

"Fine. Everyone's fine. Arthur had a little summer cold, just the sniffles. Everyone's fine. How are you?"

"Okay. Listen, Daniel, I was wondering whether you could tell me which library would be best for studying Kansas dirt."

"What about dirt, Dad?"

"I don't know exactly. Just everything."

"Probably at K-State, Dad, why?"

"K-State—" His voice trailed off.

I couldn't imagine Deal in a library. He wasn't dumb. Not at all. Just not an inside fellow. I imagined him driving up to K-State, parking his pickup, maybe getting up enough nerve to ask where the library was, looking at it a while, maybe even going inside, then deciding to turn around and go home.

"Want me to go over there with you?" I asked. "I can show you the card catalog system. It's all computerized now."

"Would you?" I could hear a huge sigh of relief coming from him or maybe I was just imagining it.

"Sure," I said. "Of course. Kansas dirt."

Chapter 15

JONAH

I watched a movie on TV the other night. It had Sally Kellerman in it, the one who was in *MASH*, back a long time ago when I was young. She was playing a divorcee who was dating about five different guys at the same time, and it got me to thinking. Maybe it was time to file for divorce and start dating five different guys at the same time. Then I thought about all the predicaments Sally Kellerman got herself into, what with one of the five guys seeing her out with one of the other five, and her having to hide herself in coat closets or wear disguises. She certainly wasn't living here because I know for a fact there aren't enough coat closets in this town to hide all the people running around. Everybody here knows everybody else's business, even if they don't seem to do the best job knowing their own and taking good care of it. Like Deal and me, I guess. I always thought we were normal and were taking care of our own business and leaving plenty of coat closets empty for other people's messes. But here we've gone and added to the general disarray: galoshes kicked out of the way so I can crumple in a dark corner with the old raccoon fur coat that should have been cleaned and sealed in mothballs for posterity. I bet Anna would have loved that coat if I hadn't let it get so ratty.

At night, when I was sick of knitting or TV, my spirits were kind of moth-eaten and sorry like that old coat. That's when running around with five boyfriends seemed most appealing.

Running around with just one boyfriend didn't seem appealing at all. My grade school friend, Hollis, for example, appeared to have switched banks so he could deposit his paycheck at my counter. If Hollis were my one and only boyfriend, he'd have been looking to deposit a mite more than just his paycheck.

Not that I ever minded sex before. Obviously, I had four kids. But the thought of getting undressed with someone other than Deal just never went very far in my brain. I would have liked companionship, but I didn't want attachment. I'd mended too many seams in my life just to have Anna tear them out on purpose to look cool, or Field stuff the carefully repaired item in a bottom drawer and never take it out at all. Attachment means you're willing to let your crushed feelings go when the children take your efforts for granted. But attachment also means you're wide open when someone rips out your heart. And throws it away.

Sometimes, after work, although I was tired and ready to drive home, I'd ease by the restaurant where Anna was waitressing. Now and then, she'd be out on the patio, setting tables for the evening meal or taking orders from a few early customers. I could catch a glimpse of her to fill my mother's heart before I went home to a clean kitchen and a clean house. If there's one thing worse than going home to a dirty house, it's going home to a clean one.

Sometimes, she'd be laughing with one of the waiters, a tall dark-haired fellow. It was great to see her laugh. I know she thought I didn't like the way she dressed, but I loved it. It was so much a part of her. True, when she was little, I tried to dissuade her from some of her more outlandish combinations. I wanted her to fit in at school so the kids would accept her. I mean, the girls wore pastel tee shirts with their jeans and tennis shoes most days, and she wanted to wear…what did she want to wear that was so terrible anyway? What did she want to wear that was so different it would have ostracized her forever? What had I truly been afraid of?

Saturday afternoon, I went downtown to Anna's restaurant. I wasn't sure when her shift started on the weekend, but I knew if I went for dinner, she'd be too busy to talk. She didn't seem to be around when I got there, and I ordered some coffee and a piece of lemon pound cake. I sat down and looked around at the young girls wearing lingerie for shirts and the young men wearing earrings, and I wondered how old I was at heart.

Then I saw her, beautiful as always, regal really, her black hair pulled back, her feet scarcely touching the ground as she brought my order. Maybe someone recognized me and told her to serve me. She set her tray down and gave me a big hug, and, God forbid, I started to cry. She handed me a napkin and knelt by my chair, patting my back and saying, "Mama, Mama." I pulled myself together, but I must have looked somewhat disheveled because she smoothed my hair with her hand and looked at me and smiled.

"I wanted to talk to you, honey," I said. "I wanted to look at you. I was hoping…I wanted to apologize. I—"

"—You wanted to apologize? You? I should apologize to you."

She sounded belligerent, and I wanted to change the subject already, but I squared my shoulders and, well, probably I gulped.

"Anna," I said. "Can we talk tomorrow?"

"Well, okay, Mom," she said. "But I have about a half hour right now before my shift really starts. We could talk now."

I was all for postponement and adjournment. I thought our legislators had the right idea. Bring a topic to the table, then table it and go out for a cigar. I gulped again and pressed on.

"Oh, honey," I said. "I've had a lot of time to think and a lot of time to rummage around that old house. For a month or so, I've been sorting through all the childhood mementos you kids collected. Cleaning house, but also saving a few precious things."

It's amazing how difficult that process is. At first, it's satisfying to fill one oversized garbage bag after another with all the broken toys and reams of smudgy schoolwork, but then it gets tricky. Do you save twenty-three trophies from each child or just one from each? And which one would they consider most special or which one would I consider most special?

"Anyway, when I got to your room, it was so neat already, like you'd strained it. It surprised me. I'm sorry, but somehow I'd missed knowing you were so…so sparing. I got to wondering what else I'd missed about you."

ANNA

Mama reached into her pocketbook and took out a small parcel wrapped in white tissue paper. It smelled like her perfume, her Mama smell, like the wild prairie roses that bordered the fence around her kitchen garden. They smother the air with their pink sweetness every summer and send out, like, engraved invitations to swarms of bees.

Mama unwrapped the little parcel carefully, placed the contents tenderly on her palm, and held it out to me. Two barrettes lay there, one still fairly well covered with multicolored glitter, the other nearly bare to the plastic.

"These were in the drawer of your bedside table," she said. "They must be pretty important."

Then it was my turn to cry and Mama's turn to comfort me.

"I thought I was protecting you from the cruelty of other kids," she said after I had calmed down a little, "but I held these barrettes in my hand a long time. I was sitting on the rug, right there by your bed, remembering when you kids were little." She shook her head and rocked back and forth. "I could see myself as a little girl, in my pigtails with little bows at the ends, trying so hard to make beautiful things."

"Once," Mama continued, "I collected clay out of a hillside to make an ashtray for my dad. I even molded the clay with an indentation on two edges where my dad could rest his cigarette. I baked it in the oven. Then I asked one of the stock clerks in Dad's dry goods store whether he had any paint. He misunderstood and painted it himself with some ancient exterior paint he found in a shed. While he was painting it white, ugh, my dad happened to see him. So when I actually presented my dad with my 'beautiful' gift, he thought the stock clerk had made it. He thanked me politely, and later I found it in the trash. I picked it out of the trash, and, you know what, I think I put it in my dresser. I don't think I had a bedside table."

It seemed like for a minute there, Mama and I connected. She seemed far away, remembering that old ashtray. Plus, I'd already showed my hand, crying. For a minute, it wasn't so scary to reach out, but the minute passed, and we hugged and half-smiled at each other.

"Bye, sweetheart," she said.

"Bye, Mama." I gave her a mini-wave as she walked away. I looked down at the barrettes in the palm of my hand and sniffed. Mmm. Still a trace of my mama's smell. Still a trace of my mama.

SUMMER
Chapter 16

WALLY

Any child can tell you right from wrong. My nephews do.

I was looking for work far and wide, even up in Lawrence where Daniel and Manya lived. I finally braved the homey thing and visited them to play the good uncle. Little Danny, he's about four, what a lover, jumped into my arms first thing, squeezed his legs around me and hugged me tight. I closed my eyes and bear-hugged him back. Manya gave me one of her famous hugs, and Ivan gave me a more tentative version. I tickled Toto. Daniel was beaming. Pater familias.

Danny took my hand and showed me around their apartment with Daniel close behind.

"Daniel, why you keeping your papers on the floor?" he asked his dad when we got to Daniel's study area. "Every night you telling me, 'Pick up your toys, Danny Boy. Pick up your toys.'" His little voice tried to pitch itself down and get gruff to mimic his dad. I almost laughed, but Manya caught my eye, finger to lips and shook her head. Later, she told me, "He sensitive, Wally. You laughing, he start to crying. He no laughing at himself yet. Not yet."

I'm not sure I'm laughing at myself yet either, and I've got a few years on him.

After lunch, I was outside playing superheroes with Ivan while the little ones napped. Ivan had on a cape that Manya must have made him from a scrap of red satin. I just had my regular bomber jacket. We were seeing how far we could throw rocks.

"Uncle Wally," he said. Ivan's brow furrowed as he picked up another rock and turned to me. "When my little brother punches me, Mama and Daddy tell me not to hit him back. They say I'm the older brother, and I know better. He doesn't even get put in time out. If I punch him, they put *me* in time out. It's not fair, Uncle Wally. Tell them it's not fair. They won't listen to me."

"I'll try, Ivan," I promised and bent down to lift his chin. "But you know what, there seems to be some rule in the world that the oldest child has to be very strong and brave because he's the oldest. There's a lot of unfairness in this world. I was lucky I wasn't the oldest."

"You could punch Uncle Field and get away with it?" Ivan asked.

"Pretty much," I said. "Do you think I should apologize to him now that I'm grown?"

Ivan deliberated a moment and said, "Yes," with all the certainty of childhood. "Yes, Uncle Wally," he said. "You should."

"Okay," I said. "Okay, Ivan, next time I see him, I will apologize. I promise. I love you, kiddo. Don't you forget that."

Like I said, any child has a moral compass that can tell you right from wrong. So why didn't Deal check his? If he checked, why did he switch north and south after all these years?

Each evening, when I got home from job hunting, I sat and licked my wounds. The more I licked, the more the heat rose.

I started reading thrillers by the night-table-full to see whether I could come up with some revenge that wouldn't come back and bite me on the ass.

I wasn't positive I actually wanted to kill Deal. Maybe just a slow torture. I thought about consulting a voodoo doctor, ha ha, but Kansas is definitely not Haiti. We do have a number of Native American tribes here and there, but my impression of them is that their witch doctors are all about healing, not the darker arts.

Then I thought that one way to hurt someone is not to hurt them directly, but to hurt someone or something they love. I shot at Deal and Dawn once. I was pretty clear I wouldn't be taking that route again.

But I knew something Deal loved. He loved his goddamn combine and his tractors with the glassed-in cabs. For years, he'd been out on the farm in all kinds of weather, and around here, we have some weather: heat up to 110 in the shade, cold down to 20 below not counting the wind chill; speaking of wind, well, you've seen the Wizard of Oz; hail that can crash into your skull like a meteor. Recently, he bought yet another new, fancy tractor with a radio and climate control. Talk about being close to the earth. That's Deal. Just loves the earth and his fellow earthlings: men…and women.

I started thinking about disabling his newest tractor item by item. First, nonessentials, like the radio, then more serious damage, like a puncture in the hydraulic fluid line so the bucket wouldn't move up or down. I didn't know yet how I'd manage it or if just imagining it would be enough for me.

Funny thing about anger. The more I fixated on revenge, the uglier I felt. Like with Dorian Gray. I had a permanent scowl on my face. My eyes felt shifty. As my secret grew, I felt kind of lightheaded. My secret wanted to take on a life of its own. I decided to meditate on my options, not act impulsively again. If I decided to get Deal, I would get him good. I might go online and download a manual for the model of his newest tractor. That could be a blueprint for effective sabotage. I'd grown up around the damn things, but I hadn't driven one lately. This new one wasn't his biggest, but it was sweet, très sweet.

Chapter 17

DANIEL

The heat was stifling when Deal parked his monster Chevy four-wheels-in-the-back- pickup at our apartment in Lawrence. I never could understand why he wanted to drive a truck with such a fat rear end. Swagger, I guess. Couldn't get more than five miles a gallon on the highway. Well, maybe eight.

Deal brought a coffeecake for Manya who didn't seem to hesitate before hugging him. "Deal," she said. "Sit. Sit. Why we never seeing you?"

Deal smiled weakly. "Hello, Manya. Good to see you." Ivan and Daniel were playing with friends next door, or they would have jumped all over him. Arthur was holding onto Manya's leg for dear life but poking his head around to check Deal out. "Let me see that Arthur." Deal tried to approach him, but he moved behind Manya to the other leg. "He walking now, Deal," Manya said. "He so good walking, da, Toto?" Manya tried to pick him up to show him off to his grandfather, but Arthur began to wail. I hugged them both, and Deal and I went out to the car.

Deal had a loose-leaf binder with him, like the first day of school, as he settled himself in my old Volvo wagon to drive to K-State. I'd had days to worry about these moments together. How would I feel? How did I feel? How was I supposed to feel? I was supposed to feel angry, I thought, but all I could feel was a jellyfish type of feeling—meaning what exactly?

Meaning, I guess, that my feelings were stinging but malleable. Meaning that love hadn't entirely melted away.

"Good to see you, son," Deal said and smiled.

He looked thin and drawn, flimsy even. I couldn't ever remember any flimsiness in his build or in his stance. Maybe he was having a few jellyfish moments of his own.

"Good to see you too, Dad," I said.

"Everything all right?" he asked. "Ivan? Danny?"

"Ship's tight as a flint," I said, wondering where the hell that language had come from. "And with you?"

"Fine, just fine," he said.

God, he wasn't much of a talker. Was I supposed to ask about Dawn or what? Should I say, "How's your love life, Dad?" or "Is Dawn better in bed than Mama?" or "How do you like living in a starter apartment? Easier to keep up than the old homestead?" So that's apparently how I was feeling: goddamn angry as hell. I settled on, "How's the farm?"

"Fine, fine," he said. "I had some trouble with the old baler a while back, but otherwise things are about where they should be for this time of year. Alden's wife was in the hospital—lumbago or some such—so there's been extra work, but otherwise not much to relate."

Fine, I thought. I will not work so hard to drag out of you what you can't be bothered to usher forth yourself. We'll just sit in silence the rest of the way. Ninety minutes of silence is not that long. But I found myself saying, "Dad, you know, you have an opportunity here. You have a son here. It's me, Daniel. What do you know about me? What do I know about you? Clearly, not a hell of a lot, or I'd have known you were fixing to leave Mama and go off with a whore. Here's your big chance, Dad. You want to learn about Kansas dirt, huh? Seems to me you wrote the book on Kansas dirt, and it's a big fucking book too. Ironic, isn't it? You, writing a book."

"I know I deserve that, son," Deal said after not such a long pause as I figured I was in for. "I'm very certain I deserve that. I do want to learn how to talk. To you. To all of you."

Deal seemed to be struggling to get that sentence out as if he had pebbles in his mouth, so there wasn't really room for words.

"I've spent my life without talking," he said. "Talking is a mystery to me."

"Thanks, Dad," I said.

"What for?" he asked.

"Thanks for trying to put something about yourself into words. Even if it's about your difficulty with talking."

"Hmm," Deal said. "Okay. Sure. It's just that when you're out on a tractor all day, all glassed in, people don't exist. Even yourself. You're just part of the machinery." Deal's voice grew so soft, I had to strain to hear him. "You know those levers like they were your arm. You don't think about which one to pull and which one to push any more. You've got a rhythm that's pleasing." He looked at me and looked down at his hands. He had his fingers opened wide. "Being with people has no rhythm at all to it. It's awkward. It's just a tongue-tying experience, being with people. In the tractor, nobody expects you to talk. But," he shook his head and paused. I might have driven ten miles before he spoke again. "You're a poet with those levers…You're a musician with that rhythm…You're an artist with that furrow. You're a man."

I didn't speak right away. That was probably more than I'd heard from Deal in one sitting in my entire life. I appreciated his effort, but it laid him bare. It was a conundrum, wanting a parent to communicate, but not really wanting to find a person behind the parent. It was more like wanting to control the conversation so the parent would talk but stay a parent at the same time. As I thought about it, it didn't seem fair of me, not very fair at all. I'd have to give this all more thought.

"Gosh, Deal," I said. But this time I wasn't calling him "Deal" to keep his Dadness at a distance. This time I was calling him "Deal" because, maybe in time, I would let him become a person to me.

DEAL

The further we drove, the more I could feel myself chicken out. I wanted to spend time with Daniel, but I didn't want to face a huge library. What was I looking for that I thought I'd find in a library anyway? I could just as well go talk to our county extension agent or go online.

"Daniel," I said after we'd driven a few more miles in silence, "You know what? I don't think I want to go to K-State today."

He tried to reassure me, but I had definitely changed my mind. My blood was pumping. My heart was beating so fast, you'd 'a thought my tractor was about to turn over on one of the grandkids.

"Let's just go on back to your place and play with the kids before I head on home," I said. "I'll work on the information another day."

I thought Daniel might be angry, but he just turned his old Volvo wagon around and shook his head.

"Sure, Dad," he said.

As we drove back toward his place, he blurted out, "You're not feeling crazy or anything, are you, Dad? You're not sick, are you?"

"I've made some foolish choices, son," I said. "I seem to have gotten kinda' impulsive here lately, I guess." I looked at the dashboard where one of the kids had scribbled on it with magic marker. Someone, Manya probably, had tried to wash it off and just managed to smear it worse.

"Maybe I am going nuts," I said. "I don't feel crazy, but I feel like some wild part of me is trying to take over. Like a tornado in June. And I am being dragged along and can't make it back to my shelter. There's tumbleweeds and old barn wood all over the place. I haven't told anyone this, Daniel, but I'd like to patch things up with your mother." I was looking down at the ravels of the car carpet. "I'm not sure she'd have me back."

MANYA

Daniel out with Deal. I singing and picking up toys. Our apartment small, but toys big. Toys everywhere and clean clothes for folding. Clean for boys and for my Daniel. Daniel papers on floor, on desk, on bed. He working too hard for us.

Toto napping, boys at neighbor. I sitting for tea in special glass with silver holder Daniel say is called filigree. Fil…Filigree. Is pretty word for lace in silver. Silver lace. Is from my homeland. Is beautiful. When drink tea, is best drink in glass in filigree. In America is everybody busy. Forget to taste. Use plastic cup. Need more silver lace. I needing more silver lace. Three children and husband. I not having time to sitting. Not stop and drinking tea. Maybe talk to doctor. Tie tubes.

Now vacuum and singing song from my Rossiya, "*Valenki, valenki.*" Rossiya living in me. "Valenki, valenki." Sometimes living so strong, I bending over missing Rossiya and Mama. But I loving my Daniel, my Ivan, my Danilushka, my Toto, so sing, sing when vacuum. Soon, heart have zip again.

Chapter 18

ANNA

What the hell, if Mama can come by the restaurant to see me and try to make up, I can go by the bank and see her. Hey, I could switch my account there and see her every time I make a deposit. Who knows what could develop? We could get to be best buds. Yeah, right.

I stood in her line right before the lunch rush even though it was slow moving. She was talking to some guy who had someone with him, could be his son maybe. They were chatting away, oblivious, and the people in the line in front of me kept switching to a shorter line 'til, finally, I was right behind the two men, and she saw me.

"Anna," she said, "What a surprise. Is everything okay?" She tried to reach over the counter to squeeze my hand, but she merely succeeded in knocking over a decoration of fake sunflowers that was in front of each teller. "Anna," she gushed, "I want you to meet my old friend, Hollis, and his son, Milam. This is my precious daughter, Anna." Mama was beaming, and all of a sudden I felt uncharacteristically shy. I was used to showing off, but I wasn't used to her showing me off...at least not in the last few years. Plus, the son, Milam, was a hunk. I mean totally.

He had on a tee shirt and jeans with a sport jacket over the tee shirt. He was maybe 6'2" and looked strong enough to lift a dancer. His dark eyes sparkled as he and his dad turned to me. Oh, man, not a dimple in his left cheek. Make that the right cheek. He held out his hand and said, "Anna, good to meet you. I'm Milam." He looked me up and down. What was I wearing? Had I fixed my hair? He said, "Anna," and he nodded his head like he was deliberating. My stomach kind of lifted and held, like continuous breathing was a new skill it hadn't nailed down yet. You could say I was smitten. I might agree with you.

"Hollis and I were in, what, third grade together?" Mama looked at him a little longer than she needed to and said, "What a coincidence he deposits here."

What a coincidence indeed. There aren't like fifty banks in downtown. Maybe there's seven or eight max. He's got to put his money somewhere. Oh crap. He's coming on to my mom. Oh crap. Oh crap. He's using the "introduce my cute son" approach. Oh holy crap.

"Good to meet you both," I said, maybe a tad insincerely. "Mama, I've got to run. Got to get back to work. Lunch rush, you know. I mean, your line was slower than I thought. You all seemed to have quite the chatting to do. See you."

Damn, just my luck. Meet the cutest guy ever, and because of his smarmy dad, getting to know the guy might give the dad more leverage to further disrupt the family unit. Damn the family unit keeping me celibate. Oh, what the hell. Fuck the family unit.

JONAH

I needed an outlet. Part-time at the bank, and the rest of my life as interesting as flat Coke. I actually used to love that about my life and the lives of all the people I knew, that they were slightly dull, simple as breathing. Occasionally, there was a wedding or a funeral punctuating the sentences of daily life, but really those were just a comma or semi-colon; there were very few exclamation points! Even my own wedding to Deal. He was a handsome fellow, and I was kind of surprised that he wanted to go out with me after he got back from Vietnam. He hadn't paid much attention to me in high school. Everybody told me how lucky I was to get to go out with this good-looking guy. I guess I believed them. I always wanted a family of my own, and losing my folks young—which was definitely an exclamation point—probably heightened my desire for a husband and kids. Well, of course, I know it did. But it also must have dampened my passion, or maybe I was just born kind of mellow…placid really…okay, passive. So I guess I married Deal because I was flattered and, also, he was a decent man. I knew he'd be steady—well, he was for over thirty years—and a good enough provider, and he wanted kids.

When I had kids, I found my passion. I wrapped up my soul in them, spread little pieces of it on each tuna noodle casserole I made, pocketed a dab in each tiny baseball uniform I washed. I glowed with each scribbled coloring they proudly handed to me before I displayed it on the fridge. Although I felt I was in many ways downright bland as Kansas, my feelings for my children sizzled with life like the sidewalks of New York, or what I imagined might be the sidewalks of New York.

I wonder if I might have tried to mute Anna's colors to make her more like me, not just so she'd fit in, but to keep her closer to home so she wouldn't ever leave me. And…maybe…also…so she wouldn't show me up for who I turned out to be.

A few days after I figured that out, I called Anna and arranged to meet her at her café before the evening shift. I was anxious again this time, but for a different reason. I had my work clothes on, a mint-colored silk blouse and darker green skirt, and my hair was cut to chin level. She didn't seem to recognize me at first when she scanned the room although she kept looking in my direction. She shook her head when she sat down and smiled.

"You look really great, Mom," she said. She kept looking at me like she couldn't quite get used to what she saw.

"Thanks, honey," I said. "How are you?"

"Pretty good," she said. "Busy. Still taking ballet and modern classes in Kansas City as often as I can afford. Working. I'm considering doing clerical work so I can have evenings free to rehearse and perform. Right now, there's no point to even audition."

"Look, sweetie," I said, "I wanted to ask you. I know you've been wanting to try New York. I have a little saved I don't need. I know you've been saving. I thought maybe I could take you up to New York, stay a week, and help you hunt an apartment. You could find a temp job, a studio to take class, maybe even audition. We could figure out the subways. I could eat sushi." I grinned. "Walk in Central Park. We could see a show."

Anna didn't say a word. She sat very still. I thought maybe I'd offended her again. Maybe New York was a project she had to approach by herself, and she just wasn't ready yet and was maybe ashamed and now would be mad at me. Maybe she thought I was pushing. Maybe our worlds were about to become untouchable again.

"Thanks, Mom," she said finally, clearing her throat. "That's quite an offer. It sounds amazing. I need a little time to think about it, but maybe we could swing it." She looked up at the ceiling and fiddled with her rings. Then she looked at me dead-on, her lips pursed. "You and me, Mom," she said. "We're pretty tough."

Chapter 19

FIELD

We were starting a development near the interstate, some mixed use: about fifty condos and town homes with a clubhouse and a pizza joint. Last fall we'd finished the model home. About two weeks ago, one of my sales guys called after showing a prospective buyer around. "Boss," he said, "there's a couple of stair-step cracks in the mortar in the basement block."

I got there as soon as I could. Not my best day. For goodness sake, the model home was brand spanking new. If it had cracks already, they could only get worse.

Brian, my construction supervisor, and I practically went over the rest of that foundation with a magnifying glass. Best we could figure, the excavation crew had dug too deep and used fill before laying the footers, so they settled, and the mortar cracked. With wet snow, the ground had expanded and pushed against the foundation wall. You could see where, in places, it had actually bowed in.

I canceled our deal with that subcontractor, and gee, can you believe it, he was not happy. That was forty-nine foundations he was not going to lay. Now he was suing me for breach of contract.

Even if I was in the right about the cause of the foundation cracks, court would mean I'd need my attorney. Court would mean days off the job sitting around waiting for judges to wake up from their naps or for lawyers to quit asking for continuances.

And you never knew, either, whether the crook might win in the end. We had documented the stair-step cracks best we could. We took pictures, wrote it all down, but you never knew what a slick lawyer might come up with. Maybe they'd say we were lying about the shoddy work because we were broke or vengeful. The excavation sub could claim it was the block layer's fault not his. And I'd have to pay my attorney…a bundle.

"Field." Brian stood part way in and part way out of my office. "You got a minute?"

"Come on in, man," I said. "What's up?"

"I been wonderin' whether I should bring this up." He was looking everywhere but at me. "That excavation company out in Iredell. The one that laid that shit foundation. We got a guy, believe his name might be Alvin."

"Byers?" I said. "You talking about Byers?"

"You didn't hear it from me," Brian said, "but his wife's sister is married to one of them Iredell bastards."

"Thanks, man," I said. "I never heard it from you."

I didn't call Alvin in right away. I wanted to get some background on B & T first. I called Wally.

"Wally," I said, "can you do me a favor? Actually a couple of favors?"

"What's up, Field?" He sounded a little sleepy. "Sock it to me."

"Well," I said, "I need someone outside my company to research another company for me. B & T Foundations. Out in Iredell. Can you find out if they have any lawsuits pending? I know you're not a lawyer. I just need some background on them. I think my estimator rigged a deal with them. I'm wondering why? And, Wally, if I have to fire my estimator, I just might need someone to go over the books with a fine-tooth comb. Someone I can trust. Think about it. You know any number-crunchers that fit that description?"

WALLY

The last thing I ever wanted to do was go to work for Mayfield Strayhorn. That had always seemed like the height, or really the depths, of humiliation when my main goal had always been to establish an independent identity to make it impossible to be overlooked in adulthood the way I thought Deal had overlooked me in childhood. Maybe my glossy life was just a variation on Anna's style. When I thought about it that way, it didn't seem so appealing. It sounded kind of pitiful actually. How do people establish their importance anyway? I figured that would be my question. Given that my previous answers had pretty much totally backfired, I decided I would just coast for a while.

So when Field called and said he'd heard I wasn't working for Old Man Sutter any more and would I like to come help him out of a jam, I thought he was just trying to soften the blow to my pride, for which, I must say, I was extremely grateful. Some of my rage flowed out of me then with an incoming rush of gratitude. Such a churning of feelings at times, I was hard-pressed to keep up with myself.

I didn't really believe he was in a jam of any kind. Not Field. Not that straight arrow. Then I was off and running mad again. It was thinking of Field as Dad's favorite that got my blood boiling. When I thought of Field as a contractor, struggling to make payroll, hoping to get a few moments with

Alicia and the kids as his payoff at the end of the day, then Field was just another sorry sap like me. If I went to work for Field, I promised myself, it would be Field the contractor I'd work for, not a rival.

All of a sudden, I missed my family desperately. As we once had been. Anna would be sitting on a high chair or on Mama's lap trying to get tall enough to reach her plate. She'd be grinning away while we tickled her. She'd be making a mess of her food. Mama would snap on a bib or tuck in a napkin that covered her whole front. I would try to throw some chow mein noodles at Field without the parents seeing. Deal would get up from the table and kneel down by me and say gently, "Son, where are your company manners?" I would try to look chagrined but would sneak a peek at Field sideways and cover up my mouth to keep from giggling. Good times. Good times.

DAWN

My mother and I were sitting around the kitchen table one night after heating up a frozen pizza.

"Why did you even marry Wally?" she asked.

"I don't know," I said. "He was cute."

"He was cute," she said. "Oh. He was cute. Jees."

"Yeah, Mom, he was. He came up to me at the Clinique counter at Dillard's and asked whether he should buy a pinker blush. I thought maybe he was some kind of transvestite or something, and I said, 'Gee, let's look at your skin color,' like I was taking him seriously, and then he laughed. He had a high-pitched laugh. He shook my hand and introduced himself as Wallace Hampstead Strayhorn and asked whether I dated transvestites. I had to laugh. He was very cute."

"So why didn't you stay with him?" Mom asked.

"Why didn't you stay with Numbers 1, 2, 3, and 4?" I shot back.

"Well let's see." Mom struck a match and lit up a Kool Super Long like she was really going to tell me why her relationships with two husbands and two halfway long-term boyfriends—one of which was my father—broke up. She exhaled, and in her old throaty smoker's voice, she said the same thing she always did when the subject came up, "Wouldn't you like to know?"

Chapter 20

JONAH

For a schoolteacher, Hollis seemed to have a lot of checks to deposit. He apparently didn't like the drive-through line or any other teller's counter.

"Hi Jonah. How are you?" he said one drizzly Monday afternoon. "You're looking great."

"Thanks, Hollis," I said looking out the window. "Not the prettiest day out there. How are you?"

"Great too," he said. "I mean fine. I was wondering, Jonah, if you'd have coffee with me one day," he blurted out, and he started rolling his checks into tubes.

"Here, let me have those checks before you turn them into pea shooters. Look, Hollis, I'd love to have coffee with you some time, but wouldn't your wife have something to say about that?"

"Aw shucks, Jonah," he said. "Tobey wouldn't mind, no sir."

"Is that right?" I nodded. "It would suit her just fine, huh?" I handed him his receipt, which he proceeded to roll up like he had the checks.

"Oh, Jonah." His teeth were practically chattering. "You know I've been carrying a torch for you since, what, when I moved here in third grade? Come on, Jonah, you're free now, right? That cad, Deal—"

"—That'll do, Hollis. Don't you dare badmouth Deal. And no, I won't have coffee or any other drink with you, that is, unless your wife would like to come along."

Hollis sighed and made a long face. "I knew you'd say that, Jonah. We're fated to be apart, aren't we? Forever. It'll always be the wrong time for us."

"Look, Hollis, you've got a beautiful wife and a fine son. What is it with you guys and mid-life anyway?"

"My Milam, he's a wonderful boy. He's good as they come. He's the top. But I can dream, can't I? Your precious, sweet face always in front of my eyes. Since third grade. I'm not kidding, no sir. You believe me, don't you? You don't think I'm here now just because I'm trying to take advantage of your recent…troubles? No siree, Bob. You know me better than that, don't you, Jonah?"

DEAL

Pastor Runkle was on the phone at his desk, but he motioned me to sit down, and I took off my John Deere cap. He had quite a few books on his shelves. Two of them jumped out at me: *The Bible in the Modern Age* and *The Spiritual Divorce.*

He hung up the phone and reached over his desk to shake my hand. "Welcome home, Brother Deal," he said. Kind of choked me up.

"Come on back to church, son," he said after we talked about the weather for a few minutes. "You know how people are," he continued. "People might be, hmm, well, frosty at first. But there are other folks'd be glad to see you. Why it might even make them feel a little more comfortable going to church with their own sins. They'd have company." I had to laugh at that. I thanked him, and we shook hands again. I rose to take my leave.

"But, first of all, Brother Deal...first of all, you need to take the Bible into consideration." His voice took on its Sunday morning resonance, and he proclaimed: "'Give honor to marriage, and remain faithful to one another in marriage. God will surely judge people who are immoral and those who commit adultery.' Hebrews 13:4.

"As I see it, Brother Deal, you've got two options, bright and clear. You can give up the harlot and return from degradation to the cleansing fires of the hearth or you can divorce God's humble servant Jonah and make your new union legal and honorable in the eyes of the Lord."

My face felt like it was on fire, and my knees buckled. I grabbed the edge of his desk so I wouldn't collapse, and I dropped my cap. "Thank you, Pastor Runkle." I could barely hear myself speak. I picked up my cap and held it across my chest, like I was at a funeral. "Two choices. Yessir. I thank you for your time."

The day I killed the red leather chair, a small metal object fell on the front walk when I took the chair out to the truck. I was awful upset that day, but I noticed a glint of silver, picked up the item, and set it somewhere.

When I got back to the apartment from visiting Pastor Runkle, I felt like a child caught with his hand in the cookie jar. I felt shamed and misunderstood, all at the same time. Children don't just eat cookies because they're sweet. Sometimes, they eat them because they're hungry too. Whose fault is it when they're hungry?

I sat on the sofa with a thud, fuming at being rejected. By a man of God who was supposed to comfort the afflicted. From a church where I'd given of myself tirelessly. The silver item, on the windowsill where I'd set it, glinted in the sunlight and caught my eye and distracted me from my self-pity. Curious, I went over and picked it up. It was an old silver pin of Jonah's, originally her mother's, I believe. It was a crane and was supposed to bring good luck.

I don't know how that pin got under the seat cushion of the red leather chair. Maybe I promised to fix the catch on it or something and had it in my pants pocket and it fell out while I was watching TV. I really can't remember. I always kind of liked that pin. For Jonah, it was a tie to her mother who died when Jo was quite young. Early on, we talked about visiting Latvia to see where her mother grew up. Once, we even got out an atlas, but that's about as far as it went.

I put my reading glasses on and took a look at that crane pin in the light. The catch on the pin seemed fine to me, pretty primitive really. It was just a piece of metal soldered onto the back of the design and arched around to hook a straight pin. Maybe Jonah had asked me whether I could arch it a little more to hook the pin tighter. I don't know.

The head and legs were plain silver, but the back and sides were layered like feathers. It didn't weigh much in my hand. I could buy some silver polish the next time I went to the store. Polished up, that pin would make a pretty surprise for Jonah. If I could get up the nerve to visit her again sometime, it would make a good excuse. After I finished the spraying, I could drop by with it. I started getting nervous thinking about it. Well, I could wait and see how I felt. I'm not sure, even with her mother's pin in hand, she'd say, "Welcome home." I miss my home. I miss my Jo.

After I polished up the pin, I found I couldn't get Jonah out of my mind. While I was out spraying grasshoppers, I saw her in my mind's eye laughing, and I had to stop and shake my head. I saw her peeling potatoes at the kitchen sink. I saw her trundling a grandbaby around while she was trying to vacuum. The visions were stronger in my mind than the spray right in front of me. I kept getting the spray volume too weak or too strong, and I had to readjust it. I figured these visions must be a sign that it was time to call on her again. I made excuses to myself for staying at the farm 'til after she got home from the bank, and then I knocked on the door.

"Hi," she said when she opened the door.

She was in a black and white sweat suit like people wear to work out.

"Hi." I was dusty from work and thought maybe I should have waited 'til I'd had a chance to take a shower.

"What's up?" she asked.

"Looks like you might be heading out," I said. "I could come back later or another time. Are you working out, Jo?"

"I'm walking, Deal, pretty much every day after work. What can I do for you?"

"Shall I walk with you, Jo?"

"I don't think so, Deal? You look done in."

"I've still got a little zip in me. I'd be honored to accompany you on your walk."

"Thanks, Deal. But right now, I'm walking alone. Maybe some other time."

"Please, Jonah," I begged. "I can't work. I think about you all day. I see you in front of me picking a big vase of black-eyed Susans in the heat of summer or washing the dog, and I can't even remember what season it is. Why, pretty soon, I'll be pesticiding the cattle and feeding the grasshoppers."

She laughed. "What do you want me to do, Deal? People can't come and go and expect you to be there right when they get back, waiting to draw them a bath or fix their favorite supper, do you think?"

"Of course not, Jo," I said. "But they could see that their man wasn't a stranger, couldn't they? They could remember that for a long time, he was a steady guy, right?"

"Sure, Deal. True enough. But think about it. What's really changed here? I've bought a sweat suit. You've rented your own place. What's really changed? If you accompany me on my walk, pretty soon you'll be moving back in, and we'll be exactly the same as before. If things had been right before, you'd have never moved out. It's a dilemma. Give it some more time, Deal. Give us some more time to grow while we're apart. Otherwise, I don't believe there's any way we can grow together."

I reached into my pocket. "I have something for you, Jo," I said. "Oh, I guess I don't have it after all. I must have left it at home." I shook my head. "I'm not exactly in my right mind."

"Well," she said, "right minds are over-rated." She gave me a quick hug. "You'll be okay. You'll be fine."

Chapter 21

JONAH

When Wally came over, it was a brisk Saturday, the kind where you wake up with energy, and your world is full of things that need doing and things that seem fun to do. I must say I was a little put out at first. I didn't really want my productive mood interrupted. Then I decided, he can just help me peel these peaches I picked up at the farmer's market, or he can sit and talk while I peel. "Whatever," as the kids say. I was going to pickle and can them for Christmas gifts. Just tie a red ribbon around the Mason jar. Something festive that would give a little kick to slices of turkey and bread dressing.

Maybe I wasn't so eager to see him because the kids, during their visits, were so darn inquisitive. They kept probing my private thoughts about Deal so they could manipulate some kind of reunion, or at least be sure I wasn't going to peel myself with a paring knife and lead to a lot of blood and mess for them to clean up. Even Alicia, when she brought the kids over, seemed to have an agenda. Manya, though, she just came to smile. What a comfort my dear Manya could be.

While her boys played, Manya and I would sit out on the breakfast nook Deal had remodeled from an old back porch that was practically falling off the house. Through the picture windows, you could see the mist rise across the field, like God drawing up a curtain on Act 1, Scene 1: Morning.

Manya would make herself a cup of tea, and she'd tell me funny stories about the boys, and we'd laugh and laugh. I thanked my lucky stars for Manya.

At first, today, when Wally came by, he didn't probe or press. He was sweet as he could be, tender even. He picked up a potato peeler right off when he saw what I had going and started peeling the skins off those peaches and putting them in the compost bucket.

I wiped some peach juice off the table covering with a sponge and then wiped it down again with a damp dishtowel. The oilcloth was starting to feel tacky. "How's it going with Field, Wally?" I asked.

"Going okay, Mama, I'm figuring out their system. Seems to be pretty sound."

"I mean, how's it going between the two of you?" I asked.

"Going pretty good, Mama." He winked at me.

"Now what does that mean?" I laughed.

"That means everything's fine. Don't worry. It means I'm on my best behavior at Field's. I've realized he and I are brothers. How about that? I bet you knew that all this time, didn't you? It's not too late for us to feel like brothers, you know. In fact, me and Daniel and him are going to go on a trip together sometime this winter. Maybe shoot some grouse." He winked again.

Field might shoot grouse, but I couldn't imagine Wally or Daniel out hunting. But hey, why not? Nowadays, it seemed anything could happen.

We filled the compost bucket full of peach parings, and I brought out a giant canning pot for more peels. The sun cast a glow on the bare peaches resting in a wide powder blue bowl. I felt soothed. Wally seemed to relax and soak up the sweet, sultry smell with a little tang in it.

"Why don't we save some of these out?" he asked. "We could have a cookout with the whole family and make peach ice cream."

"Oh, Wally," I asked. "Are you ready for that?"

"I am if you are," he said. "It will be weird, though, if everyone's here except Deal."

"We can invite him too," I said. "It wouldn't bother me."

"Whoa," Wally said. "I'm not that ready." He put down the potato peeler. "I don't believe I'll ever forgive him, Mama. You know, I don't really miss Dawn that much. I'm busy. Canoeing gets me out. Work's okay. I like playing uncle to my nephews and niece. They are a trip. I can see why you had four, Mama. I didn't think I'd ever say that. I figure if Dawn couldn't stay, better to know before the kids started coming." Wally got up and washed the sticky peach juice off his fingers.

"But for my own flesh and blood to betray me like that," he rasped. "Don't you get mad? Don't you want revenge?"

Wally paced and smacked his palm with his fist. With every smack, he emphasized his point. "I can't even beGIN to get it. It's just a line you DON'T cross. But he CROSSED it. He didn't just betray ME or you. He wiped out the FAMily.

"Like how the HELL could we even have Thanksgiving dinner together now? Even though he was only like a…a SHELL of a person, at least we had a SHELL at the head of the table, carving."

Wally's face usually looks like mine, a little scrunched up, but it was so compressed by this time, I could barely make out any features at all. I lowered my voice in an attempt at calm and tried to steer him back to a rational mode. "Shell," I said.

"Shell. I never thought of him as a shell. I always thought of him as meat. Meat and potatoes. A man of substance. But shell." I cocked my head, trying out the thought. "You're right, Wally." I nodded. "Lately more shell. A long time, actually. More shell."

Forget calming Wally down. I had to walk around too. I felt tears pricking my nostrils, and it seemed like they might move on up to my eyes. I picked up the bowl of peeled peaches and moved it over by the sink. I took the compost bucket out to my herb garden.

Did Deal really wipe us out as a family? Could he? Could anybody? I took my time working the peach skins into the soil. I looked for the wheelbarrow to haul over a load of wood ashes. As I walked by the closest tractor shed, I heard a rustling through the open doorway. "Wally? Is that you?"

I went inside and wondered, as always, how that shed stayed so cool and dark in the middle of a summer day. Its walls must have been a foot thick. I think Deal's family used it to store ice or cure meat before he expanded it for his new tractor.

"Wally?"

"It's okay, Mama, I'm just trying to work off some steam."

"You're sure you're okay? What are you doing in there?"

"I'll be out in a sec. Just give me a sec."

In the kitchen, I scraped my knife through a sharpener, cut a peach in half and threw the pit into the compost bucket. Wally came back in. "No matter what, Wally. NOBODY has the right, nobody has the power to wipe us out. Maybe the picture's changed. Maybe he's not carving at the head of the table. So. You'll carve. Or Field. Or you'll take turns. Or…" I made the mark of Zorro in the air with my paring knife. "Or I'll carve."

Wally smiled. "Oh, Mama." He shook his head. "You don't know how to carve. You're a great cook, but carving?"

He laughed. I tried to laugh. He squeezed my shoulder. That's a hug, Wally style. "How about Anna carves?" I said.

"Anna." He stepped back. "Uh huh, right." He grinned kind of lopsided. "I can see it now. The dancing carver." He nodded. "But hey, you're right about one thing. Nobody can wipe us out. Nobody."

DEAL

I see Jonah's face before me. "Jonah, Jonah," I call out. "Jonah, Jonah." Jonah's face is small and round. It just doesn't go down as long as you think it's going to. Her eyes are partly hooded, but there's a speck of washed-out blue that glints out. She wears a half-smile, almost always, kind of like the Mona Lisa. The skin on her face is very, very soft…very, very precious. There are some lines forming under her high cheekbones, but they are still gentle lines, not yet carved in deep, and her cheeks always have a tint of rose. Now her hair is salt-and-pepper gray and grown kind of wiry.

She always gave off a dreamy feeling, maybe because her eyes are partly hooded. For a guy like me, it was perfect. If she was off in her dream, I could be off in mine. When I stroked her soft face, we could be off in separate swirling dreams. Funny, how when we weren't dreaming, our worlds were as drastically real as a coffee table covered with *The Reader's Digest.* They were either so goddamn real or so goddamn filmy.

At night sometimes, before I fall asleep, her image floats in front of me, but now the hooding of her eyes seems to cast some menace. I am always surprised. They were never menacing before. I can no longer rest in my image of her. Instead I feel alarm.

I never in my life thought of Jonah as capable of harming any living creature. Well, maybe an insect. Or if, say, a raccoon got cornered and threatened one of the grandkids. I saw her chop the head off a snake with a hoe once. It took her one blow.

I lie here haunted by my Jonah, but a little afraid of her. Still, her image, even a menacing image, is more precious than, well, what have I got here? This rumpled white sheet or boxes of winter clothes stacked in the corner. Sometimes, I talk to her.

"Jo, will you ever let me back? Can I crawl back? Can I buy you a diamond ring? Will you let me sweet-talk you? They say women like their men to talk. I'm practicing, Jo. They say women like their men to play. I played with Daniel's boys the other day. They climbed all over me. You should have seen me play, Jo. They say women like their men to make them laugh. I practiced on Manya, Jo. I told her she had zip and she'd passed the zip gene on to her kids, and she laughed. They say women like to be courted, Jo. I know a field that blooms a thousand blooms. In the spring, it's covered with the green of grass waving. In the summer, you may swoon with the wheat's undulation. In the prickly fall, you know the blanket of winter is coming. It will soften the crush of your feet on stubble and thorns. It will bring you the vastness that is Kansas and could be your life with mine. Don't be angry with me anymore, Jo. Let me put my finger on your heart."

FALL
Chapter 22

WALLY

I decided to start by making the new tractor's radio inoperative. I'd studied the manual well enough at home to manage the job quickly with a pen-size flashlight. I deliberately picked a night when the moon would rise late so I could park at a distance and enter unseen. The stars were brilliant in the crisp air.

Feeling my way in the dark tractor shed brought back nights in childhood when we played hide-and-seek. Field and Daniel and Anna never seemed scared of the bogeyman, but I had the willies then, like I did now. At any second, I could bump into something or send something sprawling and make a racket. Mama might step outside and hear me or just sense my presence and come looking. I could smell the onions from her supper and the fuel oil fumes from the tank next to the house.

I remembered the gang of us, wrapped in sleeping bags, secretly moving closer together as Deal told ghost stories by a campfire. We used to sleep outside at least once a year to watch meteors blaze across the sky. At our farm at night, if you move away from the massive cottonwoods shading the house, you can see the dome of the world. Deal had built a cinder block barbecue down near the farm pond, and we would trundle our picnic supplies over there in a beat-up Radio Flyer wagon. If you've never been to a Kansas farm at night, you've never seen the night sky.

I remembered riding on Deal's lap on an ancient tractor, smoke belching. If the tractor lurched, Deal would hold me tighter and laugh and make up stories about us riding on a stallion. I never wanted him to put me down. I just wanted to keep hugging him.

Now, here I was, messing with his precious possession as he had with mine. And the stars were up there just the same, like God was still in His Heaven.

I heard the screen door slam, and my heart started pounding even more, but it was just Mama out for a second, probably throwing coffee grounds on the roses. I figured I better hurry up, though, before something aroused her suspicion or she decided she needed a tool from the shed. I heard a screech owl laughing like a hyena in the distance. They always gave me the creeps.

I started to get cold feet. What was the point of disabling the radio of Deal's tractor anyway? Would that right any wrong? Would that help me move on in my life and fill me with joy? Would that pain Deal in any way important? He'd just spend a few hours at most, probably a few minutes, 'til he figured out what was wrong with the radio and fix it. It would be a blip on his radar. But if I kept going in my plans, he'd figure out soon enough that someone was sabotaging his pride and joy. Maybe he'd even suspect Mama, but I doubt it. More than likely, he'd stake out the shed to catch me. I'd need to plan for that after my next escapade.

Well, here I was, and my feet would soon truly be cold, so I twisted the key Deal had left in the ignition and turned on the radio really low. I listened hard to make sure Mama wasn't alerted, but I didn't hear the screen door slam again. I pulled fuse after fuse out of the fuse box 'til the radio went dead. I turned off the tractor, walked back into the woods, and threw that radio fuse as far as I could throw. That felt really good, like some kind of bile got spit out of my throat. It felt so good, in fact, that I went back to the tractor shed, turned on the headlights, listened for Mama, and when I didn't hear her, I experimented with the fuses 'til the headlights went out. I walked down to the pond feeling ten feet tall and skipped that headlight fuse across the water 'til it sank. I laughed quietly and walked back to where I'd parked.

Soon, the woods path down to the road would be crunchy with fallen leaves. Quiet as I tried to be, I think I still sparked a couple of deer from their nests because I seemed to catch a glimpse of movement.

As I drove home, I watched the clouds drift across the late summer moon, blocking and revealing and blocking again, lightening and darkening the sky so the effect was one of the world breathing in and out, in and out.

It took me a long time to fall asleep. My feet wouldn't warm up even though I got up and put some thick socks on. I kept thinking about Mama all alone out there, vulnerable to whatever, and maybe lonely herself. Parents aren't supposed to be lonely. They are supposed to be models of coping, teaching us that we too can make it through hard times. I considered offering to take her canoeing one weekend but dismissed it because canoeing with Anna had been such a disaster.

After our canoe trip, I'd called Anna to check that she was okay even though I never really wanted to speak to her again. She said she was fine, not to worry, and we got off the phone quickly. I guess she didn't want to speak to me either. I couldn't imagine how we would all negotiate the holidays with one another. Forget making peach ice cream together. I, personally, was considering booking myself on a long outing with a canoe club somewhere, preferably somewhere not too cold.

A vision of my next foray into tractor sabotage emerged slowly. At first, I thought I'd progress from radio to headlight to the hydraulic line that goes to the front-end loader. But when I realized Deal would get suspicious after the second event, I knew I needed to rework my plans. I kept visualizing myself out in the dark, driving the tractor into the middle of the pond where some real damage could be done. Now that would be a gesture. I could wear gloves to avoid leaving fingerprints, and I could wear a wetsuit to stay warm when I swam out of the pond. I'd have to pick a night when Mama would be out or somehow arrange for her to be out. Hmm.

I called Daniel to set it up soon after. "How are you, Daniel? How's Manya? How're the kids?"

"Wally?" he said like he couldn't believe it was me calling. "Wally. How are you, Wally? Manya, it's Wally."

The emotion in his voice touched me, and I wondered why I didn't call more often. Well, I knew why. He was so happily married. With those beautiful kids.

"Wally," he said. "We've been worried about you, but we didn't want to pry. Why don't you come up this weekend? It's Danny's birthday. He's going to be five. Come on up and celebrate with us."

"Maybe I will, Daniel. Gosh, it's good to hear your voice." Daniel had always been the easy one for me. Daniel had this funny studious accent. Married to Manya, it had only gotten exaggerated. He almost sounded like he was Russian too.

"Listen, Daniel," I said, "I was wondering. Did you invite Mama or Deal to Danny's party?"

"Well, of course, we wanted to invite Mama, but you see Deal came over the other day and played with the kids. It's a long story. He wanted help with the library, and he ended up over here, and Danny invited him to his birthday party. We didn't know if Mama would be comfortable here at the same time. I'm afraid she'll be really hurt if we don't invite her. Come to think of it, I guess you won't want to visit while Deal's here either. God, what a mess."

"You got that right," I said. "That's sort of what I was calling about. I was over at the house the other day, and it occurred to me that it might do Mama good to get away from there some. I thought maybe you all could have her over for a long weekend. To be with the grandkids and you and Manya. Maybe she could have her own celebration with Danny so she wouldn't feel left out. You could explain about the Deal thing."

"I'm so glad you called, Wally. Of course that's what we'll do. Weekend after this, we'll have Mama spend the night, stay a few days. You could come too, if you want."

"I'm out of town that weekend. On a canoe trip," I said quickly. "I'll have to take a rain check. But I'll come up there soon. Seriously. It's important to me to be a good uncle."

ANNA

I finished my afternoon shift thinking: tonight is the night. After I got home and showered, I sat by the phone willing it to ring. I was willing Milam to call me so I wouldn't have to call him first. I sat by the phone a good fifteen minutes thinking of how he looked at the bank. How he looked into my face, and his eyes lingered there, like maybe he saw something he liked. I hadn't had a boyfriend in forever. Why now? I asked myself. Do you really want to make your life more complicated right now? While your parents and your brother are screwed to the wall, and when you think New York is just beyond the horizon? Why don't you wait 'til you hit the Big Apple and then go crazy in love? How romantic would that—then I was dialing information, and then I had his number, and then I was dialing his number, and then...his phone was ringing.

Chapter 23

DEAL

Marguerite—my only granddaughter—held on to my hand. Her little hand was practically lost in mine.

"Now don't be afraid, Grampa," she said. "I know it's your first time at my school."

"Okay, Marguerite." I grinned. "I'll try not to get scared."

Schools didn't seem to have changed all that much in the last fifty years except that the wood floors didn't creak the way I remember, and the halls, at least in this school, were lighter. They weren't painted a putrid, two-tone green. I never understood why institutional walls were painted that awful two-tone green back in my youth. Someone must have done a study saying green was the color of nature and was soft on your eyes. Something like that. That would have been enough to make the bureaucrats abandon all common sense and paint every wall the same.

Believe it or not, I *was* a little scared. Not Vietnam scared, of course, but Anna was out of college. It had been a long time since I'd been in a grammar school, and, actually, it had been a long time since I'd been in public.

"Marguerite, would you introduce your guest to us?" the teacher asked. Not really a question. Funny, how teachers do that to you.

"This is my grampa," Marguerite said still holding on to my hand but pointing at me with her other hand. "His name is actually Deal, but I call him Grampa. He is a farmer. He grows things. And he has cows. Pretty neat, huh?"

"Marguerite, what is your grandfather's last name?"

"Mr. Strayhorn."

"Children, say good morning to Mr. Strayhorn."

"Good morning, Mr. Strayhorn," they said in one voice.

"Good morning," I said.

The teacher extended her hand and introduced herself. She couldn't have been over thirty, and she might have been pretty with her even features. But there was a tightness about her I remember from my own teachers way back when. "I'm Mary Jessup. I'm so glad you were able to be with us today." She talked to me like I was in second grade too. Too bad for me. I felt like I was at least in third grade.

Miss Jessup pointed to a chair at the front of the room. A smaller chair was placed next to it. "Why don't you and Marguerite sit there?" she said. Another non-question. "We've been studying occupations. Marguerite told us that her grandfather is a farmer. We've had quite a few parents come in but no grandparents and no farmers. We've had an engineer, a professor, and a CEO so far, haven't we, class?"

Make that first grade, not third grade. Make that kindergarten.

"We're going to let Mr. Strayhorn tell you what he does as a farmer, and then you can ask questions. Mr. Strayhorn, if you would take about three or four minutes telling them what you do, maybe some of the things you grow. When you finish, they can ask you a few questions. We don't want to take too much of your time. Remember," she said, "when you talk to them, they're only in second grade."

"I've lived right here in Lyon County, except for my time in Vietnam, and—"

"—What's Vietnam?" a boy asked.

"It's a place far away. I went there a long time ago, but I've been a farmer here most of my life. When I was just your age, I used to help my father on our farm. He raised corn and alfalfa, much like I do now. Before I was born, he worked the land with a team of mules. Later, he got his first tractor. I use tractors too. Do you all know what a tractor looks like?"

I pulled out some ad photos I'd brought and passed them around.

"Be careful with Mr. Strayhorn's pictures, class," Miss Jessup said.

"You have to put gas in them to make them go," one boy said.

"Raise your hand before you speak, Tommy," Miss Jessup said.

Tommy raised his hand, and I called on him. "You have to put gas in them, don't you?" he nodded his head up and down.

"That's right. It's a special kind of gas though. It's called diesel fuel.

"On our farm, we grow soybeans and corn mostly. I farm six hundred acres of irrigated corn: the sweet corn you eat and another kind called dent corn. People turn dent corn into cornstarch or even plastic. Does anyone like to eat sweet corn?" A number of hands shot up as I passed around some samples. "What about soybeans?" A few tentative hands shot up.

"People don't usually eat soybeans just plain," I explained. "Do you know how they eat soybeans?"

"I don't like to eat soybeans," one little boy said. "Me neither," another boy said.

"Remember, class," Miss Jessup said. "Raise your hand before you speak. Let Mr. Strayhorn call on you."

"I don't like to eat soybeans either," I said. "Isn't that funny? I grow them, but I don't eat them."

"Do you grow tomatoes?" one girl asked.

"My wife grows tomatoes in her vegetable garden."

"I like tomatoes," the girl said. "They're yummy."

"Sometimes my grampa lets me ride with him on his tractor," Marguerite said. I looked at her. As far as I knew that had never occurred. "I help him grow soybeans," she said. "I'm going to be a farmer like my grampa when I grow up." She squeezed my hand.

Kids. When I used to walk to school as a kid, my friend and I would pretend about these big rocks on the way. The rocks had lines on them, some sort of different mineral embedded in the rock. We would pretend the rocks were pythons and that we had to be very, very careful walking by them so they didn't kill us on the way to school. Who could begin to imagine that in Vietnam, fifteen years later, those pythons would become real? One of them killed my buddy Derek while we were on recon. Just fell out of a tree onto his shoulders and choked him to death. When it let go of Derek, I shot it to smithereens, and there was snake blood everywhere and bits of snake.

Losing your buddy slips some gears loose inside. It's not just pythons that become real. Death becomes real. Death is no longer just a future thing. You walk around exposed and afraid, and it takes a long time to put death back in its place again. But I think the worst part of war is what you'll do in that state of fear and what you see others do in the name of your country.

One day, we were near Dak To. We had engaged in a firefight in which we had the advantage. The gooks realized they were outnumbered and slipped away into the surrounding jungle. We were going house to house to make this village secure. Women and children were standing outside, gawking at us. A lot of them looked scared. A lot of them looked sullen or you couldn't read their faces. Like maybe they were mad, but they weren't going to let you know. I remember wondering, Well, Deal, how would you feel if some foreigner had you standing outside your house with your family while they searched your property? And what would you think if the foreigner had an M16, and you were unarmed? I almost think I would tackle them barehanded, I'd be so goddamn mad. Anyway, all of a sudden, a child comes running at me. He had a bulky belt on and something in his hand, like maybe he was carrying a grenade. They used kids that way over there. Kind of like the way they use those suicide insurgents now in Iraq. They'd make the kid run at you with a grenade and tell him to pull the pin when he got close to you. Or they'd tell him to push a button to detonate his explosives belt. 'Cause they were kids, a lot of soldiers didn't suspect. They hesitated. 'Cause they hesitated, they died. I didn't hesitate. I shot the kid.

I see him before me night after night after night. I see him before me when I'm on the tractor. I used to see him coming after me in church. I'd be sitting in the pew with the whole family, sunlight streaming in through the colored glass, making rainbows in the air. I would have just said my hellos to everyone, and the preacher would have walked up to the lectern, and all of a sudden, there he was. Kid was dirty. Face was streaked. Clothes were shabby. Shirt was torn.

He took one look at my buddy and me who were getting ready to check the next hut. He started toward us at a clip, rushing us, and I didn't hesitate. After I shot him, we just kept checking those huts. Didn't find a soul hiding out or anything. No more harassment from anyone. No mothers screaming. Nothing like that. Maybe that kid was a recruit from another village or something. There was just a silence. An immense silence. Blood was rushing in my ears. Ever since, I've had this ringing in my ears. Tinnitus, they call it. The sound of that silence is deafening me. Literally. It's slowly but surely making me go deaf. And there's not a damn thing anyone knows to do about it. At least that ringing in my ears obscures silence. It distracts me from what I did over there. I don't know if anyone ever checked the kid after to see whether he was carrying a grenade. He didn't explode or anything when I shot him. He was carrying something though. I know that. He had on a belt that was super wide and bulky. I mean, those kids don't normally wear a belt of any kind. Marguerite had on a belt today in her class. Cute little outfit. Green mostly, I think it was. But with a bright pink belt. Gooks don't wear a belt.

JONAH

It was strange going into that tool and tractor shed for no reason. Even after these long, dry months, I felt if I were going in there, I should have been calling Deal to supper. Everything in its place but Deal. I picked up a screwdriver that was hanging in a row of screwdrivers, took both hands to its handle and bore down hard on Deal's workbench, pulling the screwdriver toward me to gouge a line in the rough-hewn plank. All the years he'd fixed toys or equipment on that surface, you could barely make out the line I scratched into it, and I used all my might. It felt very satisfying using my muscles to mar that workbench, but afterward, when I barely left an impression, I guess I sort of went crazy.

I started looking for other ways to make my mark on Deal's territory, and then, of course, there it was: the biggest object in this space, his newest tractor.

I was getting ready to spend the weekend with Daniel and Manya and the boys. Deal wouldn't know I'd tampered with his tractor. He wouldn't be here 'til morning. I was a nonperson to him anyway. I wouldn't do any serious damage, just cause him a little headache, that's all. Just leave a remnant of me on one of his beloved machines.

Dusk was falling, and the light inside the shed was poor. I started feeling uncomfortable in there, like someone was watching me, so I didn't turn on the overhead light. I just pulled myself up, opened the door into that tall cab, and jammed that screwdriver somewhere.

I wasn't trying to injure Deal. Truly, I wasn't. As God is my witness. He would know immediately that something wasn't right with the tractor, and when he found the screwdriver, well, then he would know someone was angry. He might not know it was me, but he would definitely know someone was angry. I would have made a mark—an anonymous mark, yes—but a mark, nonetheless.

Chapter 24

ANNA

He didn't pick up. I was pondering whether or not to leave a message. I was afraid if I left one, it would be too easy for him never to return my call. In the middle of the machine talking, he picked up. "Um," I said thrown off key for a second, "Um, this is Anna. I met you the other day."

"Anna. Oh, hi," he said.

"Um, hi." The machine kept on talking.

"Hold on, okay. The machine'll quit. Hey. Hi."

"Hi. Um, Milam, I was calling because I was wondering if you wanted to go hang out some time."

"Really? Wow. Uh, what did you have in mind?"

"Um, I was thinking, um, a beer sometime, maybe."

"Okay. How about Friday night?"

"Um, sure. Friday's good. No, wait, Damn, I have to work Friday night."

"Okay, how about Saturday?"

"Saturday. Sounds chill. Where do you hang?"

"I don't know. The Oyster? Grubb's?"

"Okay, sure, um either one is cool."

"Okay. Grubb's. Around what? 9:30 Saturday?"

"Yeah. Sweet."

"Hey, look, why don't I pick you up? I mean, it'd be a little less weird if I take you there."

"You think I'm weird calling you."

"No, come on, I didn't mean that." He laughed. "You might be weird. I don't know if you are. But you're awfully pretty to be too weird."

" Gee, thanks. I mean, if you don't want to go…"

"Anna, look, come on. I'll pick you up Saturday at 9:30, okay? Just tell me where you live, okay? "

Chapter 25

WALLY

Saturday night was really nasty. It was pouring rain, and the temperature was dropping. Sitting home and watching TV was awfully appealing. It was definitely staying-inside weather.

But having worked it out for Mama to be gone, it was also the perfect night to get that son-of-a-bitch. Screw him over. Big time. I didn't know whether I'd be finished with Deal afterward, but I definitely wasn't finished with him now.

I put on my wetsuit under my clothes and grabbed my paddling jacket and gloves. As long as I was inside the tractor cab, I'd be dryer than a taco chip. Afterwards, that's exactly what I'd do: get some taco chips with the canoe crew. Meet them for a couple of beers. I could unwind and forget about everybody's problems. I could throw away the tractor manual once and for all.

Looking from the road through our grove of cottonwoods, I couldn't spot any house lights on, but I didn't dare take a chance that Mama might be home. So, once again, I parked out on the shoulder and made my way through the woods on foot rather than driving up to the house.

The rain was on full throttle. It attacked me as I stepped out of my car, and I was quickly soaked. My tennis shoes made squish squish noises as I hurried to the shed. Visibility was rotten, and a low branch scraped my face. The wind picked up, and I started to shiver. I wished I'd added a sweater under my paddling jacket.

I still saw no lights on in the house, and Mama's car was not in the drive. I turned on my flashlight, but it made misty rings out of the rain without really illuminating my way. So what. I knew every inch of the grassy field down to the pond. I'd be fine.

Inside the shed, it was nice and cozy, and I hesitated, wondering if maybe the rain would quit if I waited a while. I reached into my jacket pocket for my cell phone. I could call somebody and chat, but I felt way too tense for chatting, and I put the phone back in my pocket. "Hey." I gave myself a pep talk. "You've got a new headlight fuse in your pocket. You'll be fine."

I flung wide the double doors of the shed, put on my gloves, hoisted myself up, and opened the door into the tractor cab. These mothers are some impressive machines. The top of the cab is probably nine feet tall. Everything's computer-controlled. I replaced the missing headlight fuse and took a deep breath. "We're going to do this thing, baby," I said to the tractor. I turned the key Deal always left in the ignition, and the engine purred to life immediately. No messing with a diesel heater, no delays. I turned on the climate control and the windshield wipers. Better not to put on the seat belt. Easier to exit once I plant this iron monster in the pond.

Slowly, I moved out into the driving rain. Deal had left two giant round hay bales on the front forks of the tractor. Those babies each probably weighed upwards of a thousand pounds. Soaking those in the pond with the tractor would just add to Deal's problems. Super!

The headlights were working fine, but the bales blocked them from casting much light up ahead. What light seeped through was blurred by the rain into those mesmerizing rings. I raised the hay forks above the cab so I could get more illumination. As I proceeded, I picked up a little confidence. Cockiness even. Hot shit, here I was, in the air comfort seat with the heater turned up, so high above Mother Nature in Deal's fucking tractor. And I knew every root and rut. Hell, it was my home. Deal's farm, but my home. I'd fucking lived there all my fucking life.

The rain turned to hail. First, little pebble-sized bits, then, golf ball-sized chunks. I could hear them knocking on the cab glass and on the paint. No matter what other damage occurred, Deal would not like the dents in that ever-startling John-Deere-green finish. I wished I could rock out with the radio blasting, but I didn't bring a replacement fuse for the radio. I tried to turn on a CD, but he must not have had one in there. I wished Deal would let me drive this tractor in the day so I could really check it out. Maybe it wasn't just Deal who'd never been interested in me. Maybe I'd never shown an interest in his world either.

Winters of freezing and heaving earth had left the ground uneven, and it was stippled with rocks. Plus, we have gophers. The hail was quickly turning the wet grass into an ice rink. I picked up some speed. I rumbled across the flat field behind the house toward the gentle slope that leads to the pond. "I get it, Deal," I said. "Every day, you feel the massive power of these mighty machines. You got the idea you were the Terminator, huh, and not a damn human being? I'll show you, Deal. Hasta la vista, baby."

I felt a spring in the tractor's step, like a lumbering old mule feeling its oats. "You better slow the fuck down, Wallace," I said and hit the brake. I must have turned the steering wheel too. The tractor spun across the grade. The manual said I'd be safe inside if the tractor rolled as long as I used the seat belt and the state-of-the-art roll bar it came with. But damn if I was going to be stupid and stay in there waiting to be pinned. Before I could open the door and jump, the tractor fell on its downhill side, and I was thrown hard against the inside of the cab. I smashed my head on who knows what, and my right arm was cut, but the tractor was not on top of me. Thank you, God. That thing weighs like ten thousand pounds without a load. I must have lost consciousness for a few minutes before I managed to get a foothold on the edge of the seat, grab the tractor door with my left hand, open it, and pull myself to the outside of the tractor. I was sitting pretty, although soaked, figuring how to get down when I realized my head was turning like a merry-go-round, and I fell to the soggy ground.

A searing pain ripped through my right arm. Something was definitely wrong. I should have worn a paddling helmet to protect my head from all this hail, but at least I had my wetsuit and gloves on. Okay. Let me get my cell phone out. I just need to unzip my... Ah, look…at…those…little…green…grasshoppers play…

ANNA

I watched him from the window pull his rain shell over his head while he opened his umbrella, which promptly turned inside out. He made a mad dash for my apartment. I checked my new top in the hall mirror.

"Anna," he hollered and pounded on my door. "You in there? It's crazy out here."

I opened the door, and he came in, took the shell off his head and shook it. He stared at me.

"What?" I asked.

"Damn," he said.

"Rotten night."

"No," he said. "I mean, yeah, it's rotten, but that's not why I said damn."

"Oh." I shook my head. "Why'd you say damn?"

"Honestly," he said, "you just kinda' took my breath away for a minute."

"Oh," I said.

"Your hair was backlit from the hall. I don't know. That purple sweater. It's like you've got gauze on over it."

"It's organza," I said.

He looked around.

I followed his eyes: posters on the walls. CD's on a shelf. A sofa. A coffee table.

"Nice place," he said.

"Thanks," I said and grinned. "Ready?"

Grubb's was too hot and too smoky. The band was too loud. I could hardly hear a word he said. I know he couldn't hear me even though I was pretty much yelling. He kept saying, "What? Huh?"

"Look," he said. "I know this is probably a stupid idea, but what if we went back to your place? I could pick up some beers. Or wine. Whatever you like. What do you think? I'd like to get to know you a little, and I have no idea what the heck you just said."

"I'm not sure I heard you right," I yelled.

He motioned to the door with his head and lifted my coat from the chair to put over my shoulders. "Come on," he said. "Okay?"

He repeated his suggestion in the car.

"I guess so," I said. I must have looked at him kind of funny.

"It'll be fine," he said. "It's fine if you don't want to. We could go to the Dunk 'N Dine?"

"The Dunk 'N Dine?"

"Anyplace. You know. A diner. Whatever. Someplace not so loud."

"It's fine. You can come over. I've got some wine if you want."

The weather had not improved in the short time we'd been inside, and I thanked God for umbrellas as we ran to Milam's car. At one point in the slow drive to my apartment, we were attacked by hailstones.

"Your poor car," I said. "Lucky, it's not us."

"Amen to that," he said. "To both of those. Tonight, the deluge. Tomorrow, the dent doctor."

When we finally made it to my front door, he motioned me to enter first.

"Get in here," I said. "Get out of that monsoon while I hang up my coat. Are you soaked? Do you need a towel?"

"Do I need a towel?" He touched his hair. "Maybe. Sure. A towel would be great."

I brought a towel and ruffled his hair with it.

He took my hand and drew me over to the sofa and set the towel on the coffee table.

"Did anyone ever tell you how beautiful you are?" he asked.

"Nope," I said. "No one ever did."

"Let me be the first," he said. "You are beautiful. Smashingly, disturbingly beautiful."

"What about weird?" I asked.

"Beautiful and weird," he said kissing me lightly. "Extremely, excellently weird."

DEAL

Sunday dawned bright and clear, but debris from last night's storm lay all over the road. I had to stop twice on my way to the farm to move a tree limb. When I neared the driveway, I saw a car like Wally's Audi parked out on the road with some hail dents and some small branches on it and almost drove away again.

But last night, with the storm coming, I'd left two, half-ton hay bales on the tractor spears when I'd run out of daylight. I needed to get them into the barn. More importantly, I needed to check the corn and bean fields for hail damage. I was trying not to think the worst, but my mind was racing: I could be wiped out.

Even if Wally had spent the night, I was pretty sure he'd be sleeping in late, or at least he'd ignore me. But why had he left his car on the road? That didn't make much sense.

Wally's sleeping in, and I am consumed with worry. As I turned into the driveway, I thought, why in the heck do I keep working as a farmer? The debt I carry is a crushing burden. It is hard to imagine that a small family operation like mine has over a half million dollars in equipment to maintain not including barns and outbuildings. Then there's seed and feed and charges for fertilizer and insecticide and herbicide. There's incidentals. Fences. Gates. You name it.

Back when the kids were small, there was so much purpose in everything. Waking the kids up on a cold morning at the end of winter to watch a calving. Imagining that some of them would be out there with me when they grew up, driving the truck while I ran the combine for the harvesting. Going to a farm equipment auction together. It all just made so much sense. If I kept the family going by bringing in an income, eventually, they'd help. One day, they'd take over the major part of the work, and I'd help. It would be part of the natural order of things. I was keeping my parents' land in the family. The land was a living heritage. It could be forever. Time was just an illusion.

But so much has changed. Where my dad could make a living off of sixty acres and a tractor, I've got his acreage plus a thousand more. I've had to add onto his land to have a prayer of making it on this farm. Right now, I've got three tractors, one that's taller than some rooftops. I've got a 12-row planter, a combine, a baler, a pickup, and a semi. I've got a hundred head of cattle. And with all my hard work, all my investment, some years the weather does not see fit to cooperate, nor the government, nor the middleman, nor the consumer, and I operate at a loss. I don't complain, but when I'm all to myself, I call this farm "Hook, Line, and Sinker." Not Bar-S Ranch or Strayhorn Acres. Nothing traditional like that. Hook, Line, and Sinker. That's the name of my place. Kansas may be mostly flat, but I'm always driving my tractor on the edge of insolvency.

Plus, it's a lonely life. Except for the help I hire spring and fall, I'm out there on my own, day after day. I had four kids, but none of them are out there with me. Not even for the harvest.

When Jo and I were together, after the kids left, there was still a heart in it. There was still a home to come home to. There was still a reason for my back to break with the labor and with the worry. We could give Wally a down payment on his first house. That was satisfaction. We could get the crib for the nursery when Field and Alicia's first child was born. We could offer to help bring Manya's mother over for a visit from Russia. There was still the feeling of being more than just me. I was still connected to the generations forward and back. I was plugged into the land, the family, and maybe God or Jesus. But now, the land just seems like an object. I work her like a mule. She shuffles along or she kicks back. God...who knows? Or cares. God and I seem to have parted ways some time ago. So why do I keep being a farmer? Who the hell am I kidding? What the f... else would I know how to do?

I can't say I don't still love my land, object that it has become. And I'm not aiming to put it up for auction like so many do in desperation. And, damn it, when all else fails, I still love Kansas. The other night, I worked late, and I was driving back to my apartment. Long dark clouds moved against the darker sky. The sky was a dome that covered all my land, my thousand acres, spread out as it is. I've lived here in Lyon County my whole life, except for Vietnam, and I love the way that dome sky at night makes you feel. The sky around here goes from forever to forever, but it can barely contain Kansas. It was the kind of night that makes you feel humble and grateful to have any place at all on this earth.

I drove up the driveway, noticing new ruts gouged in the gravel from last night's storm. The doors to the shed for the new tractor were open, and the shed was empty. There were tracks in the long, wet grass. Heart in my throat, I followed the trail down to the pond where I saw my beautiful machine lying like a dead animal, two wheels up in the air. There were hail craters in the finish. The hay bales had rolled off. The headlights were still faintly warming the morning mist.

Then I saw Wally, pale as death, lying in the grass, a few feet uphill. I rushed to him trembling. His pulse was weak, and his breathing was rapid and shallow. He had cuts all over his face, and his right arm was cut to the bone. I grabbed my cell phone and punched in 911. "Hurry," I screamed. "It's Deal Strayhorn near Homestead on 111 between T and U. Hurry," I said again. "It's my son. He's hurt bad. Tractor accident."

"Give us five minutes, Deal," they said.

"I'm gonna' get a blanket to warm him up some. Hurry. You'll see the tractor tracks in the grass behind the house going down toward the pond. Follow those tracks. He's hurt bad."

I raced back to the house, which was locked for some reason. We never locked it unless we went out of town, but I found the key under the mat. I grabbed a few blankets out of the linen closet and ran back, the smell of cedar deep in those blankets. I believe it was Wally helped me line what was once an old pantry with the cedar planks so long ago. Jo had always wanted a cedar closet so she could forget the mothballs.

Wally looked about the same. The ground was soaked with blood. Maybe he didn't have any blood left because the cuts I could see were dried or just oozing slightly. But that couldn't be right. He'd be dead if he didn't have any blood left.

I was trying to think. What did we do in Vietnam? I piled all three blankets on him. When someone faints, you can elevate their feet, but I didn't dare. Better not to move a person at all. They could have a back injury.

I put my hand on his good shoulder and started talking. "Wally, you're going to be fine, son. You're going to be all right. You've been a good son, Wally. You've always been a good son. I'm so proud of you, Wally. I've always been proud of you. You're a good boy, Wally. You're a wonderful man, my dear son." I couldn't break down. "You'll be fine, Wally. Just hang on. You'll be fine, son. You'll be fine."

Two First Responders jumped out of their truck. One got to work on Wally while the other called the ambulance on a hand-held radio. My mind must have been jumbled into grasping only fragments. "Multiple system trauma. Exposure of unknown duration." The other first responder, a female, checked Wally's airway. I heard "fracture" and "blood loss" and "hypothermia." "Suggest air transport."

"Ambulance is on its way, Deal," the man said to me as the woman started to suction Wally.

The ambulance arrived in what seemed like forever, but I think it was in a flash. It fishtailed a bit in its rush toward the pond, but it stayed upright. The paramedics took over. I felt unnaturally calm. They cut his wetsuit from his right arm, gave Wally oxygen and stabilized his neck with a brace. Several people started to set up a landing zone in the pasture.

I heard a whirring, taketa-taketa-taketa from a helicopter overhead, and I felt its wind. I was back in Vietnam in my worst nightmare waiting for a fallen buddy to be medevaced from a firefight. Although the morning was still cool, sweat drenched my shirt. I was afraid the helicopter and I would be hit by hostile fire.

"Wonder what he was doing wearing a wetsuit, Deal?" one of the paramedics asked me.

I shook my head. "Huh?" I said. I shook it again and saw Wally. Wally. He was so pale.

"Pretty good protection from the weather, the way it was last night," the paramedic said.

"He's lost a lot of blood," another one said.

They started IVs.

They stabilized his right arm with a vacuum splint and log-rolled him onto a spine board. There was a pad under his head, and foam blocks were strapped on either side to keep his head from moving. They lifted the board in a synchronized manner and loaded Wally onto the helicopter.

"Where are you taking the bird?" I asked. "I mean, the helicopter."

"Wichita or Kansas City," one of them said. "Do you have a preference?"

"Which one's better for Wally?" I asked.

"They're the same, Deal," he said.

"Then Wichita," I said. "It's a little closer."

"Okay," he said. "Wichita it is. Wesley Medical Center. Gather up your troops and meet us over there. Don't drive crazy now, Deal. He'll need you."

After the helicopter took off, I just stood in the grass for a minute looking at the blood, the tractor, bits of safety glass everywhere, and the bales of hay. Wally must have climbed out after he lost control of the tractor. He wasn't crushed, but he might still die. Best to get out of here and get to Wichita. Call Jonah. Where the hell is she?

I pulled myself up onto that fallen tractor, reached in the broken cab window and, with fingers, which were becoming thick and stiff, awkwardly turned off the headlights, the heater fan, and the ignition.

I called Daniel first. He'd already left for some peace and quiet at the library, but Manya said she could reach him. Jonah was at their house. Thank God. That's where she'd gone. Of course, why wouldn't she visit her grandkids if she wanted to?

"Manya," I said. "Wally's been hurt. He's headed for Wichita…Wesley Medical Center. We don't know anything yet. Would you put Jonah on, please?"

"Jonah, honey, sit down, will you? I've got some bad news. Wally's hurt. He's being medevaced to Wichita. I'm going there now. We don't know anything yet."

"He's not…? " she started to ask.

"Oh no. Oh no. God help us, no."

"What—"

"—Tractor accident. See if Daniel can drive you. Ask at the information desk where they've taken Wally. I'll be wherever they say."

I repeated basically the same conversation to Alicia. Field was already out, but she'd get him on his cell. I left a message for Anna to call me.

I hope I will never again have to repeat a trip like the one to Wichita that day. I could keep the car on the road, but I knew every moment I didn't belong behind the wheel. It was like I was a figment of my own imagination. The faculty of judgment had escaped me. I smoked some pot in 'Nam and drove a jeep once when I was high. It was just like that. You have to get your conscious brain to substitute for the part that's usually automatic. You have to remind yourself over and over to keep that conscious part on. Kind of like when you're falling asleep at the wheel, and you keep slapping your cheek to stay awake. I wasn't falling asleep. Not by a long shot. But my whole self was praying for Wally, and there wasn't enough left over to be driving. Wally, Wally, Wally, Wally. God, God, God, God.

A nurse in the emergency room told me they were prepping Wally for surgery and told me where to fill out the paperwork. She offered me a cup of coffee, which was awfully nice of her. I just wanted to buy a pack of cigarettes.

I couldn't figure it out. Why was Wally driving the tractor in the first place? Why was his car out on the road on a night as crazy as last night? And he'd been dressed funny. The paramedics had asked why he was wearing a wetsuit. They said that might have saved him from dying of exposure last night. Exposure to the wet and cold and a massive loss of blood. Oh my God.

JONAH

I wanted to fly to the hospital, but if I couldn't fly, I most certainly didn't want to wait around for Manya to find Daniel. I'd been painting with Ivan and Danny in the den. We'd had breakfast, and Manya was getting the baby ready for a bath. The kids and I had been content sitting on their scratchy shag carpet. They had little smocks on. When Deal called, my fingers were smeared with red. Daubs of black stained my shirt. I didn't have a smock, but I should have put on an apron or something.

A part of me was like a first grade teacher, talking to myself, reminding myself how to pick up my purse and overnight bag nonchalantly so as not to frighten the children, how to hug them like I meant it, and how to put one foot in front of the other in order to walk to the car. The first grade teacher helped me find a key in the rubble inside my purse and told me how to insert it into the ignition.

Normally, the drive home takes over an hour, sometimes an hour and a half, but I had to make it all the way to Wichita.

"It'll take awhile," I told myself. "Just keep your eyes on the road, your hands on the wheel. Your right leg pushes the gas pedal and touches the brake when need be. You watch for traffic. You watch your speed. You don't get in a wreck. Your only job is to get to the hospital."

I can't say I was nervous right then. The limited faculties checking in with me were too busy remembering what a steering wheel was for. Possibly the rest of my faculties were nervous, but I didn't have access to them.

Deal was standing in the surgery waiting room when I walked in. Several other people were scattered around the room in what looked like family clumps. Deal came toward me and put his hands up, fingers splayed. He looked like he was trying to show a cop he didn't have a gun or something.

"They took him to surgery," he said. "He's already in surgery. They were going to do a CT scan of his head and neck and x-ray his arm. They wanted to know if I was the decision maker. The decision maker. Because he's separated from his wife. Can I get you something, Jonah? You look like you might faint."

Deal took hold of my hands to lead me to one of the sofas. "Jeez, Jo," he said, "your hands are freezing. Can I get you a cup of tea?"

I wanted to drift away into oblivion and wake up and be back on that scratchy shag carpet at Daniel's house, painting with the kids. "Maybe in a minute," I said. "What happened out there? Maybe I better sit down."

"He broke his right arm," Deal said. "He lost a lot of blood. I don't know if he hit his head or not, but, hell, how could he not have? But he was breathing, Jo. He had a pulse.

He's young. He's strong." Deal's face was red. He seemed to be radiating heat.

"I saw his car on the road near the driveway when I arrived at the farm this morning," Deal continued. "Tell you the truth, I hesitated before I went on up the drive. I was scared I'd have to see Wally. Thank God…can you imagine if I hadn't had the nerve to go up to the farm? Nobody would have found him 'til Monday." Deal started to tremble violently.

"I did one thing right, Jonah," he said, barely audible. "I got up the nerve because I was afraid of the hail damage. The new tractor wasn't in the shed, but you could make out tracks in the grass. I don't know how it was up at Daniel's last night, but down here, we had a terrible storm: howling rain, hail. Golf-ball-size hail.

"I followed the tracks 'til I saw the tractor down near the pond. The tractor was on its side. He must have been going pretty fast or swerved to avoid something and hit the brakes. Visibility was probably near to nonexistent last night.

"When the tractor started to flip, he must have been thrown inside the cab. Those heavy bales on there. Oh God, the hay bales. I left the hay bales on there. Oh Jesus. It was my fault. It was probably all my fault. If only I'd put the hay in the barn last night. Looked like Wally raised those hay spears up too high, and they destabilized the works."

"Deal, my goodness, you can't possibly think this was your fault because of the hay, do you? Because—" But before I could tell him what I'd done to the tractor myself, he cut in.

"—Sure it was, Jonah," he said. "It *is* all my fault. All of it." His red face turned white, and he began to cry. Hulking sobs. Wracking sobs. I fished in my purse for a Kleenex and handed it to him. After a few minutes, the sobbing ebbed. He wiped his face and looked past me into the distance of the sterile waiting room, the irrelevant TV high on the wall chattering, the other families shrinking in on themselves. A spasm periodically engulfed his body.

"What have I done, Jonah? What have I done to us all? To my family. My dearest family. To you. To my precious son. My funny little Wally.

Deal put his hand against his mouth as if to keep the truth from escaping and bit down hard on the inside of his middle finger. He jammed the knuckle of his index finger in his mouth and bit down.

Deal shook himself out of his trance and spoke in a pleading tone as if he could somehow stop the events of last night from having happened. "Why did he go out there last night? Why on earth did he take my tractor out there?"

"I can't imagine," I said. "On a night like what you said too."

"He had on a wetsuit," Deal said.

"He wears it for canoeing sometimes," I said. "When the water's supposed to be really cold. In case he comes out of the boat."

"Well, I guess, he was planning to go paddling today," Deal said. "But that still doesn't explain why he was out in the rain last night driving the tractor, does it?"

"No, Deal," I said. "It doesn't."

Deal put his head in his hands and mumbled something I couldn't quite get.

Daniel and Field arrived. They pulled up chairs in front of us, and they held my hands really tight. "Wally?" they asked. "What?"

Deal pulled himself together and brushed his eyes against his sleeve. "We don't know yet," he said, some color returning to his cheeks as he took on a once familiar role. "They haven't told us anything yet." The three of them talked in hushed tones although there were no longer any other folks in the room. I retreated into a numbed world of my own.

After a long, long time, a young doctor approached, and we all rose as he introduced himself. "Dr. Talbot," he said. "Just got out of surgery with Wallace."

"I'm Wallace's father, Deal Strayhorn, and this is my wife, Jonah, Wally's mother. These are our sons, Mayfield and Daniel."

The doctor shook hands all around. "Please, sit down," he said and pulled up a chair. "Wallace will be in the SICU shortly. He's strong, but he lost a lot of blood. So far, we've given him two units. In addition, he sustained severe lacerations to his right arm and had an open fracture. We affixed a titanium plate and screws to the humeral shaft.

"He also suffered a serious blow to the head, and we're going to monitor the intracranial pressure closely."

"But how is he?" Deal asked. "Is he going to be all right?"

"Frankly," Dr. Talbot said, and we all held our breath, "it's touch and go right now. Too early to prognosticate. But, as I said, he's strong. Comes from good stock, I see." He smiled at us.

Neither Deal nor I smiled back. We were leaning forward, ears pricked, as if we could pick up signals from the doctor or from the waiting room walls that might tell us how Wally was. If signals were being sent, I couldn't hear or read them. I doubt Deal could read them either.

"Actually," Dr. Talbot continued, "he's unresponsive right now."

"Unresponsive," Field shouted. "What do you mean? Like a coma?"

Dr. Talbot gave one of those tolerant smiles that pretend to be empathetic but really are just waiting 'til you calm down. "Not exactly like a coma," he said. "We see no evidence of a skull fracture or stroke, but the CT scan shows evidence of cerebral contusion. That could be why he's unconscious. It could take time to resolve. He could have headaches. We might or might not have to operate. As I said, we'll be monitoring him very closely. And it could take weeks or months before we know how much nerve damage his arm has sustained."

"You mean his arm might not work?" Field shouted again.

"It depends on how much soft tissue was damaged," Dr. Talbot said. "In the large majority of cases, the arm returns to normal functioning. It will take two months for the bone to heal, but he should get motion in about two weeks."

"When can we see him?" I asked.

"Once we get him settled in the SICU. You can see him then."

Waiting in a waiting room. Not all rooms are so aptly named or so universally capable of being sized up in one quick glance. The terror I felt when Deal first called had subsided with the boredom of waiting. Now it returned with a vengeance. My heart was in my throat, and my heartbeat was racing. I felt if someone touched me, my entire body might burst into a shower of sparks. My head took on a life of its own and focused on breathing life into Wally. You'd have thought I was a Hare Krishna for the mantra I kept repeating to myself: "You can make it, Wally; you can make it, Wally; God, help him make it; help him, God."

After about forty-five minutes, a nurse appeared and beckoned. "You all can visit," she said. "You can sort out how many want to come in now. He's not awake yet. The doctor will be back up shortly."

I went in first by myself. Wally's right arm was covered with a cast and bandages, and he was hooked up to various hanging bags with fluids in them. A monitor had lines zigzagging across it. He was on a ventilator and was covered with a warming blanket, so there wasn't all that much of him visible. Just being in the room with him was a comfort, though, because I could talk to him, and I could send him my wishes for his healing more directly. Plus, I could hear the haaw haaw whee sounds of the oxygen and know just when each breath was pumped in. He had to be alive if he was breathing or, well, being breathed.

"Wally," I said, "it's Mama. I love you, honey. You're going to be fine. We all love you, honey. You're our wonderful boy. Just take it easy and rest, honey. Take your time." As I stroked his left arm, I resolved not to let my mind play with "what ifs." I will stay in the present as much as possible and keep sending positive energy to Wally, I decided, but maybe it's okay to ask God once to bless us with Wally's recovery. I didn't want to second guess God or bargain with Him (or Her). I didn't want to be a pest. I sent up a brief request. "God, consider your servant, Wally. Wally is a good man. He needs You right now if You can swing it."

My conception of God had changed quite a bit over the years. Maybe because of Anna's cynicism or the influence of the long view that Daniel took. I wasn't really clear on how and why my conception had changed. I still found comfort in a community of lost souls huddling together in church, and I liked the hymns and familiar routine. We also had a very nice preacher. But God was no longer a masculine protector to me. She-He-It was more of a seasonal ebb and flow. I felt God when I watched the birds at the feeder on a winter's day. I felt God when I didn't have to redo too many rows of knitting but got a rhythm going and saw color and pattern unwind from a single skein of yarn. I saw God in old photo albums. I wasn't positive God was back with Wally yet, but I didn't think pushing Her-Him-It would do any good.

While Deal and the boys took their turns with Wally, I tried Anna and finally reached her. "Anna, sweetheart, Wally's in the hospital in Wichita. Deal and the boys and I are here. We've been trying to get you. All the tests are not finished, so we don't have all the information on how badly he's hurt yet. Can you come?"

"Oh my God, Mama. Is he going to be okay?"

"They don't know yet, honey. We don't know much yet. I just got to see him, but he's sedated and kind of out of it. He hasn't woken up yet."

"What happened? Never mind. I'll call work. I'll get there as soon as I can. Anything I can bring for you?"

"Bring your Bible, honey, okay? I think I'd like to hold it."

"You can hold my hand, Mama, but I'll bring the Bible too. I know I can find it somewhere."

Then there was nothing to do but wait with Wally. Listen to the whees and beeps and clicks that had nurses coming in to check and revise the settings. Periodically, one of the boys or Deal would sit by me and squeeze my hand or put their arm around my shoulder. Periodically, I did the same for them. Anna came and brought the Bible and was very good. She joined in the periodic hugging and squeezing and didn't make a fuss. Someone went for coffee. Someone went for tea. Around late afternoon, we all decided to take a break from our vigil and find a decent restaurant to build up our strength for whatever might lie ahead.

Chapter 26

WALLY

When you sleep, you cannot dream; when you dream, you cannot sleep. Even as the thought whispered itself through my aching head, it didn't make sense. Aches. Sense. Mysteries all of them. I returned to Never Never Land, not the place I had imagined in childhood that Wendy and Peter would go. This was a place of rhythms and beeps, all different kinds of beeps, sometimes clicks, and a steady haaw haaw followed by a whee. Maybe I was in a cereal box and children were breaking it down to get the toy out. When it got peaceful, they were maybe just stopping a while to slurp their milk and read the comic on the back.

Something was in my throat. I should try to get it out. Sometimes, there was pressure, light pressure on my arm. I only had one arm. I saw the other arm in heaven the other day. God only knows what He wants to do with my arm in Heaven. Maybe Jesus needs it. "A good right arm," Jesus says to His children. "You never know when you'll need one."

Sometimes, I felt love enter the room like having the chickenpox when you're a kid, and Mama bathes you and puts lotion on you and lets you watch TV all day wrapped in the comforter from her bed.

Mostly, haaw, haaw, whee.

"How about some threesomes?" I say to the noises. I try to ask for haaw, haaw, haaw, whee, but pretty soon I'm just lying in the fog, cold rain dancing on my face.

DANIEL

"Manya, You guys all doing okay? Everything fine?"

"Da, da. Okay, okay. But Wally? What is, how is Wally?"

"You're okay. That's a relief. I've been so busy worrying about Wally, I started worrying about you guys too."

I stepped outside for a minute to call Manya on my cell. It was unseasonably hot and overcast. Possibly building up to another storm. If I were at a pay phone, I'd be trying to wind that stiff metal phone cord around and around, which it never would do. I picked up an empty cigarette pack off the sidewalk. I tried to twist it one-handed. Of course, I couldn't.

"They don't have much info about Wally yet," I continued. "How can they not know anything? If I'd spent three hours operating on somebody's arm, I'd know the ins and outs of that arm pretty well, I would think, wouldn't you?

"I mean, when Danny busted his knee jumping off the swing when it was so high, didn't you get a good look at the insides of his knee before you got him to the hospital? What was inside it, sweetie? I don't think you ever told me. Gee, I don't want him to get hurt again, but I wish I could see the inside of his knee sometime, to know him inside and out. Is that a little nuts, honey? I think I'm going a little nuts sitting here.

"I know you were worried how everyone would be sitting in the waiting room together, waiting. We didn't dare think about Thanksgiving, did we, and now, here we are, all of us but Wally, of course, he's in the other room. You're not here, my love, and the kids aren't, and Alicia and their kids. But the principals of the Strayhorn clan, we're all here like a family should be to honor and protect in time of crisis, and we don't even seem weird to each other. We seem fine. No wonder I'm a little nuts, Manya.

"Field and I just whisper with Deal. I've never whispered so much in my life. It's very conspiratorial, but we're just talking about the weather and the crops. Deal may have suffered terrible damage from the hail the other night. He hasn't had time to check. Field mentioned some legal problems. Just his mentioning a problem of any kind is a revolution, don't you think? You know Field, honey. He never has a problem, right?

"So I told them about my dissertation committee requiring my investigation into that new statistical method they don't even teach in our department. I have to get someone from the math department on my committee, they said. Or sociology. Now, when I'm almost done. Sociology. Oh my God. I have to start the analysis over with that other method that they don't even know how to do. Sorry, I'm raising my voice. I forgot to keep whispering. It's going to cost us at least another semester. 'Grin and bear it,' Field said. He's right. What other choice have I got, sweetie. He grins all the time. It's killing me.

"You have to go, don't you? I can hear Toto crying. Is he getting up from his afternoon nap? Go give him a sippy cup, honey. Tell him his Papa loves him. I love you, Minxie, give Danilushka and Vanya a big hug from me. I'll call later, Manya. I love you, honey. I'm talking a mile a minute. I must be tenser than I thought."

"Daniel, I hugging you on phone. Daniel. How going Babushka? She okay?"

"Yah, we're all taking care of Babushka. Anna's being good too."

"Oh, is good, good."

"Do you need anything? You're okay? I don't know how long we'll be here. Can you last? Maybe get Connie to babysit for an hour so you can get a break. I'll call you soon, my *daragaya.* I love you, *milaya.*"

JONAH

Monday morning, daylight seeped between and around the slats in the blinds and cast soft shadows on dear Wally, beset with bandages, catheters, lines and monitors. I was sitting by his bed chanting my little love chants, trying not to barter with God, transmitting as much love and physical warmth through my fingers on his as one person can offer to another when Wally slowly opened his eyes. He was already off the ventilator, and his lips moved toward a smile, lightly as if they were trying on the smile for size. "Hi, Mama," he said. Then he closed his eyes again. I thought he might be dead, and my heart stopped. But no, his chest still rose and fell. He was still breathing. I felt his wrist. Still a pulse.

I rushed to the nurses' station to report. "He woke up for a minute. He said, 'Hello' to me."

A dark-haired nurse came out from behind that counter they hide behind and patted me on the arm. "Good news," she said. "That's a good sign, dear."

I went into the waiting room. Daniel and Anna were sleeping, the Bible on a chair next to her. Field was on his cell. Deal sat with his head in his hands. He was trying not to make noise when he cried. I sat down beside him and put my arms around him. Awkward, a chair arm between you and the one you hug.

"He woke up, Deal." I had tears in my voice. "He said, 'Hi, Mama' to me. The nurse said it was a good sign. His breathing is slower. Deal, his brain is working enough to say hello."

I kept hugging Deal. His shoulders were shaking. His chest was heaving against me. His tears wet my blouse. He no longer tried to keep quiet. His cries rumbled through that waiting room. Relief and remorse, I guess, all mixed up together and letting go. The others must have heard him and woke up. They came over and put their arms around both of us. Field must have gotten off the phone. "Wally woke up," I told them, my voice muffled in all the arms. "He said hello."

Chapter 27

FIELD

My bro. Let me tell you about my bro. I have two of them, of course. But there's something about the one right next to you on the stair steps, always about to catch up but never quite able. Fast as you run away from him or push him down, you change your mind and want to stop and take his hand, help him catch up, teach him to grip a football, throw one too.

Wally was my first kid. The other sibs, the hell with them, let them manage somehow or maybe they'll take care of each other. Who knew, who cared? I don't really mean that. I love them all, even Anna. But it was Wally and me before it was Alicia and me, before it was Alicia and me and the kids.

So I helped him out with the job thing.

He would have done the same. In fact, when I told him about the lawsuit, he told me he had a little money saved if I needed it.

"You know how lawyers are," he said. "Money-grubbing sons of bitches. Near as bad as accountants." He laughed.

Wally kind of giggles when he laughs. He's not the most masculine guy. Funny, he's compact, so he actually looks kind of like Deal in a way. But then again, he doesn't. Wally's nose has more of a bulb on the end, his build is more scrawny, and he's sweeter. Except for his temper, he's nearly as sweet as Daniel. Deal and me, we're the hard asses. Well, that's our image anyway. Got to keep up your image.

Not long after Mama told us that Wally had said hello, the doctor came out again. What a sight we were. Not much image at that time. Rumpled, actually. Quite the day and night, we'd had there. Kind of amazing when you think about it. We were still a goddamn family. Kinda' shocked the shit out of me that we took back up where we'd left off before the Deal & Dawn thing. We were all there for the same reason. We loved Wally. He was ours. Still to come, of course, whether Wally would even let Deal into his hospital room. Didn't matter. Wally was going to make it. He was fucking going to make it.

"Looks pretty good," the doctor said. "Wallace is resting peacefully now. He's regained some color. His breathing is steady. It may be months before we know what his arm will be capable of. And," the guy paused. He seemed like a nice guy. He seemed like a competent doc, but when they pause, you think they've seen too many movies, and it drives you crazy. You want them to spit it all out. Tell you really fast like those fast-talkers on TV telling you one by one in ten seconds all the side effects of Prozac, but take it anyway.

"And," the doc continued, "we don't know whether there'll be any problems from the cerebral contusion. As I said, it could be months before we know exactly what damage has been done. What we do know is that there's a good chance he's going to celebrate Thanksgiving with you all this year, and he needs a lot of rest. So get some breakfast, and then go home and get some rest yourselves. You're an impressive family group," he said. "Wally must be very proud."

Ah yes, would that it were so. Rumpled as we were, our image was working magic on that fine doc. The only bad thing about Wally waking up was that we might dissolve again as a family. If our closeness set him back, if it made his recovery too anxiety-ridden, we'd have to relinquish our ties to keep him on the mend. Better just go get that breakfast this morning. Who knows when we'd be dining together again?

JONAH

Wally was sleeping when I snuck back into his room for a minute. He had color in his face again. The warming blanket had been removed, and he had a regular hospital blanket on. I could pick up some toiletries for him tomorrow after I finished work. Maybe get him some PJs. The god of cataclysm had seen fit to spare us this time. The god of peace was tingeing Wally's cheeks with rose.

Did you ever think that watching the rising and falling of someone's chest as they breathe was a sacred act? We try so hard to be productive: planting, tending, harvesting, canning. We try so hard to say the right thing, keep the car tuned. And all we really need to do for those we love is sit by them in a dim light and watch their chest rise and fall.

ALICIA

Field went by work before he came home, so it was Monday night before I finally got the whole scoop. He was exhausted, and I made him a drink, Chivas straight up, then another. I had the gas logs burning. The kids were in bed. He told me what they knew about Wally's arm and the cerebral contusion, which I didn't comment on, having started in nursing in my former life and knowing more than I wished about what that could mean for Wally's faculties. At least, Wally could talk, and his body was recouping for now.

When he told me about the family at breakfast, I started to cry. My family, my non-family, was a joke. Alcoholism ran through my family on both sides like a flood. It swept them away without any rescue boats around, Mother and Father perpetually drowning. Two sisters swam away as far as possible to find solid ground. One became a nun in South America with some Indian tribe. The other was a hippie in California. She never drank. Just took mescaline, LSD, Ecstasy, smoked a little weed, slept around. Who lives in a commune in the year 2004? My sister. She renamed herself Tourmaline and forgot to answer calls. She said she was her own crystal.

Field was my answer to that crew of mine. I planned to reinvent the concept of family with him. He was a rock, very basic. He was a contractor, for God's sake. His drinking was for making contacts or after a rough day. The bottle of Chivas stayed in the liquor cabinet. It didn't travel with him.

I married Field for himself and for his family. I don't think I had any illusions about him. I didn't want excitement. But when Deal took off, I realized any hope of day breaking each morning with the family circle always intact was an illusion. I was shattered back to childhood despite my relentless efforts to stay far, far away.

Chapter 28

WALLY

It was dark when I woke up. I was in a strange room. A dim light was on. Machines beeped periodically. Why did those sounds seem strange but familiar? A nurse came over. Why?

"How are you feeling, Mr. Strayhorn?" she asked me.

How does she know my name? "Gee, let's see," I said. "By the way, who are you, and where am I, and why are you here?"

She laughed. She was kind of cute. Little, like Mama. If it was the middle of the night, why was she laughing?

"I work here," she said. "I'm Amanda. This is the SICU in Wesley Medical Center. In Wichita. You've been in the hospital nearly twenty-four hours. You've been on this unit since after your surgery yesterday morning."

"Surgery," I said, "what surgery? What day is it now?"

"You really ask a lot of questions," she said, but she didn't seem to mind. "It's Monday night. You got to the hospital yesterday morning. They operated on your arm and inserted a catheter to monitor intracranial pressure. They gave you blood. You'd lost a lot of blood. Since then you've been here. I've been watching you, um, sleep, off and on, since I got on. The nurses told me at report that your family was here. They took turns visiting you. They said you have a big family."

"I do," I said. "I have a great family."

When you come up from underwater after going off a high dive, it's always kind of a miracle that you know how to breathe air so automatically. You don't have to relearn every time. I guess I was breathing. I guess I was breathing unless I was in heaven, but it didn't feel automatic.

"Tell me, um, Amanda…what was the surgery for?" I asked, kind of like I was curious about somebody else. "Why had I lost all this blood?"

"According to your chart, they had to mend a compound fracture. That's why you have a cast on your right arm. You can lose a lot of blood from those. Lucky…Ah…The paramedics brought you in. Some kind of accident, I guess. The writing wasn't so clear. Looked like, 'tractor,' but maybe they were saying something else."

"Tractor," I said. "Tractor? What would I be doing on a tractor?" I looked at my right arm. Sure enough, there was a cast on it. She wasn't lying about that.

"Don't know, Mr. Strayhorn," she said.

"Call me Wally," I said. "Everyone calls me Wally."

"Don't know, Wally. Maybe the doctor can clue you in later this morning. Or definitely your folks. They can fill in the gaps for you when they come by. Too bad, I'll probably be off then. That's the problem with the night shift. I don't get to meet a lot of families, but I can talk with the patients, right?" she smiled.

"Right," I said. I tried to smile, but my face was stiff.

"I think I'll take a nap 'til the sun comes up," I said. "Um, is the sun still coming up pretty regular?"

"Don't worry," she said. "Last I knew, it was still coming up every morning." She put her hand on my cast briefly. "You get some rest," she said.

Chapter 29

DEAL

I sat up all night. Most of the night I held the silver crane pin from Jonah's mother in my hand and prayed. The pin was a little rough. It reminded me to pay attention. I wasn't a Catholic. I don't know that I'd ever been up all night praying.

One time, when Field was little and had a high fever, we stayed up with him all night, putting cool cloths on him. Numerous times, Jonah was up walking the babies I know, but I was probably passed out in the bed. Many times, Wally, or was it Daniel, I think it was Daniel, had the night terrors, and we'd take turns tending to him. He'd scream so loud, even I couldn't sleep through it. But praying? No. Praying was for in church on Sunday morning when the preacher said, "Let us pray."

I found a little carved candle. Dawn must have brought it over when she moved in. It was very pretty. Red, with little curlicues all over it. A shame to burn, but I wanted a ray of light while I was praying. I set it upright on a plate on the windowsill in the front room and knelt by the window. If I'd found some incense, I think I would have lit it too. It would have kept me company through the night.

I put my hands together like a child beside his bed saying his prayers. "God," I said over and over, "thank You for saving our Wally. Thank You. Thank You. Thank You." I guess that's what they call a mantra. Every once in a while, I took a sip of cold coffee, walked around the apartment, pulled my hair.

After a long time, I moved to the sofa and sat, kind of like a rag doll. I must have dozed off or entered an altered state of some kind. It was like I was watching a newsreel of the last few months, and the main character was a guy that looked a lot like me.

The guy had on a John Deere cap, and his skin was tanned pretty dark. He worked his fields on a good-looking tractor pondering: what on earth was it all for? At the end of the day—this is the part that killed me—the man got plowed under like a failed crop. The next day, he was out there again, working away, and at the end of that day, he got plowed under again. The scene of him working and being plowed under played and replayed. I dreaded the next replay like you do a nightmare that has too much truth in it. The poor man was barely alive. He couldn't feel his outsides. He couldn't feel his insides. In the newsreel, the characters of the man's family were like shadows in the background. They were barely visible. They tried to send messages to the man, but he couldn't hear them. He couldn't remember how much he loved his wife and children. He couldn't remember they were the world to him. He could just remember that at the end of the day, he was going to be plowed under again.

And then, in the newsreel, he busted out like a torpedo. Actually, it was more like his body busted the rest of him out. His mind was stuck in the replay, but his body refused to be plowed under ever again. His body busted out with these tentacles that glowed. The tentacles touched everything around him. They were highly sensitive. Sensitized. As they snaked along, they vibrated with the dust on the furniture. They polished the finish on his tractor. They teased the down on the thighs of women who were not his to touch. The man could feel again. He wanted to keep feeling so bad. He reveled in feeling. He gorged himself on feeling. He waved at the shadows that were his family. "Go away," he yelled at them. "Go away."

When the sun came up, I felt like I was trying to crawl out from underground like the man in the newsreel. I clawed my way out of the sofa and gulped the air. My head was splitting. I took the point of Jonah's silver pin and raked it across my palm. A line of blood. A new life line. I looked at it for a long time. The blood dried and got hard. "God." I heard my voice croak. "Please, help me find a better way."

I splashed cold water on my face and rubbed it hard with a towel. I scorched some coffee, sloshed it down my throat and felt it burn. I hiked up my dress pants and headed off to the SICU. Nothing could stop me from trying to see Wally. I knew there was a high probability—I guessed about eighty or ninety percent probability—he'd bar me from visiting. If he did, it might actually kill me, but I was going to try to see him anyway.

I tiptoed into Wally's room. He was up having breakfast. He didn't send that little table on wheels flying across the room when he saw me, so I moved a little closer to his bed.

"Mornin', son," I said. "How are you feeling?"

"Whew," he said. "No doubt I'm alive is there? Every piece of me hurts some way or other. Otherwise, hungry. This food hits the spot. I could go for some cornbread or biscuits though. Maybe a little red eye gravy. I bet I could mop up a few biscuits this morning if they were offering any."

"Tell you what," I said. "I'll go hunt you some if they'll let you have 'em. I don't see why they wouldn't."

"Did Mom come over with you?"

"Uh, hmm, she'll be over shortly is my guess."

"Good. That's good. Have you seen Dawn?"

"Uh, Dawn, uh, no. Not for a good long time. Did you want Dawn?"

"Well, I thought she'd be here with me, seeing as I'm in the hospital."

"Dawn," I said. "You know the nurses had us try to call her when you first got admitted. I think Field called her mother's. Her mother is a colorful woman. She's not sure of Dawn's current location, Wally."

Wally looked at me kind of funny. Puzzled, angry. I couldn't quite read his expression. His memory was clearly fuzzy.

"Wally," I said. "You've been through a lot in the last thirty-six hours. Actually, we weren't positive you were going to make it, son. No matter what you think of me, son, I'd like you to let me stand by you through this. Whatever it takes. Whatever that means. Until you get back on your feet."

"You're my dad, aren't you?" he said. "Of course, I want you around. I just have to figure out how to get in touch with Dawn 'cause she's supposed to be here, right?"

"Okay, Wally. Of course."

"Then I'll get her mother's number from Field. He'll be coming by, won't he?"

"Of course, son. Field was here all day Sunday. So were Daniel and Anna and your mother. They were all worried sick about you. Alicia and Manya would have come too, I know, but they were watching the kids."

"Those are some crackerjack kids," Wally said. "Dawn and I are going to have kids one day. Dad, how did I get in here? Can you fill me in?"

Wally has this way of poking out his lower jaw. It's one of his main expressions. I've seen him use it when he was confused or nervous or angry. I've seen him use it when I thought he was going to cry. His jaw was doing a lot of poking out. I kind of wished I'd stuck that silver pin in my dress pants this morning so I could grab hold of it.

"Wally." I paused and sighed and sighed again and shook my head. "Wally, I was going over to the farm Sunday morning to work. The new tractor was not in the shed, but there'd been a terrible storm the night before, and I could see where the tractor tires had mashed down the wet grass. I just followed the tracks. They led down toward the pond. The tractor was lying on its side. The lights were still on but barely. A few paces away, there you were, unconscious. Blood everywhere on the ground next to you. Your right arm was all torn up." I looked at Wally to see if I should continue.

"Go on," he said in this cold, cold voice that sounded like it came from a robot far away.

"You had a wetsuit on under your clothes," I said. "I guess you had planned to go canoeing later. That wetsuit may have saved you because it was awful out Saturday night, rain and wind, big hail."

A shiver went through Wally's whole body like watching the wind blow a ripple clear across the pond.

"I ran up to the house. The door was locked, but the key was under the mat. I called 911 and grabbed some blankets to cover you 'til the paramedics could get there.

"That's pretty much it, son." Wally's jaw was not poking out at all. I could not tell what he was thinking. "They medevaced you here. I called the family, and they all came as fast as they were able. Then we waited, and the doctors and nurses did the rest."

"I guess you better leave now," the robot person said. "Better you should leave."

"Okay, son," I said. "If that's what you want. Okay."

I stumbled out of that room and into my truck where I just sat. It was mighty cold out, and I did turn on the engine to get some heat. My breath fogged up the windshield. No one who happened by could see me weeping.

WINTER
Chapter 30

JONAH

Wally's hospital room felt like the inside of a metal cargo unit, not that I'd ever been shipped in one. It was comfortable enough to be sure. Sanitary. Temperature controlled. But, there was a metallic taste to everything, like swallowing liquid aluminum for some medical procedure.

"Hi, honey," I said. "How are you feeling this morning?"

"Just great, Mama," he said. His tone was chilling. He didn't sound like Wally at all.

"Is everything still hurting, honey?" I asked.

"Not at all," he said, still with that chill.

"How's your arm?"

"It's fine. It's in a cast, isn't it? It has to be fine in there. I can't see it. I can't feel it. My arm's better off in the cast where it belongs."

He could talk, thank goodness. Faculties intact. Maybe he'd be able to walk too. But where, just where, God, did you put my Wally?

Wally stayed in the hospital for a week. The medical staff was amazed at his quick recovery. "Good genes," they said. "All that canoeing," they said. In desperation, I talked to the hospital social worker once. She was very reassuring. "This happens sometimes. PTSD and TBI. He'll get over it. Just give him some time. I can give you some counseling referrals if you'd like."

"Maybe so," I said. "I'll call you."

He came home with me. There was no way I was letting him go home alone in that state. I was hoping that he could soak me up over time, take the chill off. He never mentioned Dawn. He never mentioned Deal.

Deal called one day, incoherent. Whatever it was, I didn't help him clarify. Field closed up Wally's house, drained the pipes. I think Deal helped him.

About a week later, Wally went back to work for Field, but he kept living with me. He rocked a lot in my refinished rocker. He stayed in his old bedroom, fingering the models he and Field had made as boys. He walked in the snow when it came. He ate like a bird and lost, who knows, maybe ten, fifteen pounds. He wasn't fat to begin with. I tried to make over him on Thanksgiving and served a turkey breast with the fixin's. He picked at his colorful plate: the harvest orange of sweet potato casserole, the yellow gravy drizzled on the bread stuffing and on the white meat, the fresh green of string beans. He ate a little cranberry sauce.

The only time Wally warmed was when Alicia or Manya brought the kids over. Then he seemed to forget to be encased in that cargo unit. He got down on the floor with the kids in the family room and played for hours. They built towers out of blocks. He played horsey and bumped them around on his back. He helped change Toto's diaper or gave him a bottle. I tried to get the girls to bring the kids as often as possible, but they were busy too. They had lives, and their kids had lives, and their husbands had lives. They could only come over now and then.

Anna was a peach. She knocked herself out. She came over, probably two or three times a week. Although Wally held himself stiff as a board, she hugged him really long. She rubbed his back. While he rocked, she pushed the sofa back some and danced for him. I left them alone in there, busied myself with tidying up or writing Christmas cards or whatever.

Wally never spoke about the tractor, and I didn't ask. It wasn't time to ask. I hoped there would be such a time. Anna and I weren't headed to New York any time soon either, or at least I wasn't. How had I managed the needs of four when they were younger? I could barely manage Wally and myself now.

It was funny how broken I felt after Wally came home. I'd done so well after Deal left, relatively speaking. Of course, I'd had moments, but over all, I'd picked myself up, dusted myself off, and headed up the road. Now Wally's ghost made the house into a vast cavern. No matter what I did—build a fire in the fireplace, wash the kitchen curtains—my efforts echoed through empty space and refused to fill it.

Chapter 31

ALICIA

I decided that one way to help Wally forgive Deal would be for Dawn to take the blame for everything. I didn't know whether Anna would be up for this one. It seemed a little far out even for the two of us. I don't know, I guess I had fantasized me and Anna as puppeteers who could pull the strings of life and get the little puppet family dancing together again.

Anna was less consumed than I was by the puppet project. She was more distracted. For one thing, she still had mixed feelings about her family. After all, they were *her* family. It's usually easier to be captivated by someone else's family than your very own. You find these hollows in another person's family that enfold you and make you "a part of," and you don't want to get up even to go to the bathroom. Also, I had the kids, and I was busy, but I was settled. Anna still had her whole life to figure out although I think she'd started dating "the son." Plus, when it's your own family, don't you sort of tend to take them for granted? For background music? Or take sides and miss the big picture?

So I decided to go out on my own limb this time and not even tell Anna. I remembered Dawn's mother lived in Missouri. I'd met her at the wedding, and we'd chatted, if you can call it that. She did most of the talking. At that time, she lived in Kansas City, just over the state line.

I checked her out on the web. Got a name, address, and phone number. Mrs. Marjorie Dawes. Yup, that's right. Dawn was born Dawn Dawes. A good reason to marry if you ask me.

I told Field I was going to Kansas City to do some Christmas shopping while the kids were in school and asked him to pick them up in case I was late getting back. Monday morning, I took off. I thought I might have to bum around all day 'til she got home from work. I couldn't remember exactly where she worked, but then I thought, hey, maybe she's a cocktail waitress or something and works nights. She seemed like a cocktail waitress. Tight to absurd-fitting clothes. Hoarse smoker's voice. Classy.

Mrs. Marjorie Dawes was indeed home. I drove by and saw her walk by the front window. Drapes were open. Car in the drive. I called her to ask her whether she'd mind my coming by. "I came over to Kansas City to do some Christmas shopping," I said. "Feel like having company?"

"Why not?" she said. "Come on over."

She lived in a little brick ranch on a modest but clean street. Better than I'd expected, really. Her house was very neat inside too. Yeah, it smelled like smoke, but the ashtrays were emptied and wiped out. No overflowing butts. She offered me a cup of coffee, and we sat in the living room. Pictures of Dawn were everywhere. As a beautiful child; Little Miss Kansas City Pageant participant; Junior Miss Roundup Second Runner-Up with a cowboy hat, lariat, and fringed short, short skirt; as a cheerleader; Homecoming Court; wet tee shirt contest. No wedding dress. Pretty, pretty girl.

"Cut to the chase, Alicia," she said.

"You don't mess around, do you, Marjorie?" I laughed, trying to keep it light.

"Cut the shit," she said. "What do you want? You and that old faggot father-in-law you've got. Why Dawn could still be married if it weren't for that old prick. She might have a kid by now. I could be the doting grandmother."

"Mrs. Dawes," I said. "I'd like to speak to Dawn. None of us can trace her without your help. We tried when Wally was in the hospital. You wouldn't help us then. He almost died, you know? We've tried online. Wally never hurt your daughter, and he's suffering right now. I don't know that she could help, but the way I figure it, she owes him at least to try."

"Don't you figure anything Dawn could do would just rub it in, Alicia?" she asked.

"It might," I said. "You're right about that. But what if she visited him just one time and said she was sorry? Could you just give me her number and let her decide for herself?"

"Now, Alicia, that is something I cannot do," she said. "I see where you're coming from, you little bitch. Put it all on my daughter. My beautiful daughter. Make her to blame for that old fart's horny ways. Quite the church-going family you have there. Did he put you up to this? Is he boffing you too, huh? You're almost as pretty as Dawn, aren't you? He likes them young and pretty, doesn't he, huh? Does he want to be knocking over every cute little thing? Can't he pick on someone his own age, like maybe his wife, huh? She's probably frigid, isn't she, huh? Why doesn't he just pick a farm animal, huh? He's a farmer, isn't he, huh?"

I was out the door by then, imagining the last part of the diatribe, not really hearing all her words. What kind of life could a person have that would make them have a mouth like Mrs. Marjorie Dawes? My skin crawled. I smelled like smoke all over. Thank God, I hadn't gotten Anna to come with me. I needed to air out, bad. I drove to this big park they have in Kansas City, a sculpture garden, and I wandered around. Some of the pieces were under wraps, renovation or something, but a bunch of them were still on view. Henry Moore pieces. Amazing. Renoir, Rodin, and huge badminton birdies all over the place. They call them shuttlecocks. Crazy. When I'd heard about them, I'd wanted to see them. I'd wondered if they'd give you the feeling that even if you get batted about from time to time, and you're currently stuck on the ground, you can be okay. You can take wing. When I saw the shuttlecocks, though, they just seemed immensely heavy. Pieces of concrete in the shapes of badminton birdies. They didn't look like they could ever fly.

Still, the brisk air washed the smell of smoke off of me, and I felt reasonably proud of myself. I'd done what I could to honor my vow to get the family back together. I'd made it through a visit to a scary, ugly lady, and now, here I was in a sculpture garden. What if I took a sculpting class to take my mind off the Strayhorns for a while, give me some time to figure out my next plan? That could be really fun. Maybe I could get Wally to come with me.

I was smiling as I drove back to town. Christmas shopping be damned. It could wait. It would get done. It always did. I was looking forward to picking Marguerite and Allen up from school. I called Field to tell him I could get the kids. He sounded tired. "Thanks, honey," he said. Even if I couldn't fix Field's family, I had created a beautiful family of my own. All of a sudden, something moved inside of me, kind of like rearranging the furniture, and without any doubt, I knew that I could stop my scheming. Field's family would have to put themselves back together without me…or not. It wasn't my job any more.

WALLY

I'd been lazing around Mama's for a while. My arm was mending but very weak and slightly withered-looking. Apparently, I wasn't going to die real quick, and I wasn't going to be a vegetable. I limped a little on my right side, and I had headaches from time to time. The doctor said to expect a few bumps and bruises. After all, they all kept saying, "You nearly died."

How did they know? I'm too ornery to die, at least bodywise. Soulwise is another matter. I've been feeling on the order of dead here lately. The nurse at the hospital called it PTSD and TBI. They all think I suffered a lot. I give. They can call it suffering. But I tell you what I call it. I call it hatred festering.

Deal's out and about around the farm at least six days a week. I block out any sounds of his tinkering. I heard he got the tractor going again. He keeps the driveway plowed. But you know what? If he were to have a tractor accident, I wouldn't lift a finger to help him. Even though he saved my life. I'd let him die in agony.

At the same time, I'm not interested in activity. I can make it to work. I do the minimum. I do the dishes for Mama. I sleep. Oh yeah, I do some sleeping. Ironic isn't it? I went to all that trouble to get over here to screw up his beloved tractor, and now I'm here full time, and I don't give a shit about his goddamn tractor. Also ironic is the fact that I tried to destroy something precious to him, and all I destroyed is myself. Additionally ironic is the fact that it appears I *am* precious to him, or why else would he have saved me? It isn't just Field he cares about. Not just Dawn. He also cares about poor little old me.

Why the fuck did he shack up with Dawn then? Why did he want to destroy my life? It just doesn't make any sense.

Chapter 32

DEAL

Everyone did their own Thanksgiving. Alden, who's worked for me off and on forever, invited me, and I went. His kids are grown and gone, and he's a proud man. Proud and humble. I've known him and his wife my whole life, but I'd never been to their house before. His wife fixed a lovely meal. I was surprised they fed me without judgment. Not a lot of questions or conversation either for that matter. Some talk about the weather. Plans for me to make my welding equipment mobile and make some extra cash by helping out my neighbors in winter when I'm idle.

Most of the time, I feel like I picked up the wrong size nut at the hardware store, and it won't thread on this old bolt. Still, I'm trying. I've gone to watch two of the grandkids, Field's Allen and Daniel's Ivan, play soccer. It's a miracle to stand on the sidelines and see mini-generations, some who've emerged from your own seed running around. We clap and yell. We're thrilled when Allen's team actually runs toward the right goal.

Alicia and Manya are kind to me although I'm not sure why. Each of them is a good person in her own way. Manya is very straightforward. She's a large woman, but she uses her size as warmth. She'll just hug you to death. I could see she might set someone straight if she put her mind to it. "I know you good man," she said to me last time I went up there. "I know it." Oh, that Manya. She about killed me.

Alicia is very pretty. I get the feeling she's hiding something a lot of the time, but it never seems threatening. Field is, well, Field. Daniel's a little distant still, but kind enough. They haven't taught their kids to hate me. Those kids'll jump all over you if you let them. I feel like Santa Claus. I vaguely remember that phase with mine. I know I let some of them sit on my lap on my old tractor. The boys, maybe. Anna, I don't know.

Chapter 33

MANYA

I giving Toto bath other day.

"Manya, milaya," Daniel telling me every day, "Don't say, 'I giving Toto a bath.' Say, 'I gave Toto a bath.'"

I gave Toto a bath.

He not staying still. He slippery with soap. All of a sudden, he under water, and I panicking and screaming. I grabbing him and hugging him. I all wet, and he crying. I drying him and rocking him, and he stopping cried and smiling. I giving—I gave—him a nap. Phone ringing, and I running to phone and slipping on wet floor and falling and hurting knee. I thinking, no more children. No more.

What is perfect number? Four? Square? Three? Bozhe moi, the Trinity. I crossing myself. I crossed myself. I not cared what number is perfect. For me, three is perfect number. No more children. I visit, I visited doctor. He tell me, "You young. You strong. No tying tubes. But if you want tie tubes, is $3500." Where I get? Where I get?

I love my *malenkie detishki*, my Vanya, my Danilushka, my Toto. I love Daniel. I no wanting more. So many little ones hungry in world. I feeding my children. I good to other little ones. World is not needing more children. I is not. Daniel tell me, "Manya, just say you're fresh out of zip. Then I'll know you need a break." Daniel working so hard for us. I not saying to him, "Daniel, I fresh out of zip."

God, you not my friend right now. Why you bring baby inside me again? I go every week: vespers, church, taking my malenkie detishki, my little ones. Other day, I feeling so—how you say—desperate. I want get coat hanger. I look on Internet: "How To Do Home Abortion." I order kit. "Low cost. No risk. Sterile. FDA-approved medication. No surgery." Is perfect.

I follow directions. I take pill. Today, another pill. I go—I went—to bathroom. Toto napping. Danilushka at pre-school. Vanya, my big boy, at school. I put special pills from kit inside me. Pills burning. Okay, pills doing job. Directions saying, "Put pills in. Then lie down." I lie down, but burning so strong, I going back to bathroom. I letting cool water in bathtub. I try washing my inside. Not helping. Still burning. I getting very hot, very cold, very hot, very cold. Blood coming. Blood means baby coming out. Is good. No more children. More blood, more blood. Water pink. Water red. I sad for baby. I needing toilet. I never liking green floor. Too dark. Ugly, ugly. Now green floor turning, turning. Green walls turning. I must not to fainting. If I fainting, who watching Toto when he wake up? I getting pad for blood. I holding on to wall. I going to kitchen, slowly, slowly. In kitchen is beautiful picture of Virgin, Bogorodica, from my mother. Is gold. Is blue. Bogorodica understanding Manya even if God not understanding. I crossing myself. Bozhe moi, I holding on to chair. Phone, where is phone? I calling Daniel. Mobile ringing and ringing. "You have reached the mobile phone of Daniel Strayhorn. I'm sorry I can't take your call at the moment. Please leave a message, and I'll get right back to you." I no leaving message. I calling Alicia. She not home. I no want call Jonah. She working. She sad. Anna. Mobile is ringing and ringing. "Hi, it's

Anna, leave a message, and I'll get back to you pronto." I calling 911.

WALLY

The hospital called Field's office. Field was out, and his secretary transferred the call to me. I was rummaging around Field's desk looking for some papers he'd asked me to go over. In the middle drawer was a small envelope with Dawn's handwriting on it. "Wally," Field's secretary said. "It's the hospital. They wouldn't tell me what's going on." I put the note in my pocket.

"Hello," I said. "I'm Wallace Strayhorn. Can I help you?"

"Mr. Strayhorn," the woman said. "We're calling about Manya Strayhorn. What is your relationship to her?"

"I'm her brother-in-law," I said. "Is something the matter?"

"How can we get in touch with her husband?" she said.

"I'm dialing him as we speak," I said, "on my cell. Has something happened?"

"I'm afraid we have bad news. His wife has been in an accident. We're not at liberty to divulge any information except to her husband."

"Oh my God," I said. "Where are the kids?"

"What kids, sir? The EMTs made no mention of children."

"She has little kids. They would have been with her, at least the baby would have been with her. Maybe the other two are in school. Hey, just a minute, her husband just walked in.

"Field," I said, my hand covering the telephone receiver, "pretend you're Daniel. The hospital's calling about Manya, and they'll only talk to Daniel. I'm trying to get him on the cell."

"Hello," Field said, "this is Mr. Strayhorn. What's going on?"

"Sir," the hospital said, "your wife's had a serious accident. Please, come as quickly as possible."

Field inhaled sharply and grabbed at the top of the desk, knocking some papers off. "Of course," he said. "Thank you. I'll be right there."

"Serious accident," Field said when he hung up. "That's all they said."

"Daniel," I said when I reached him, "sit down. Bad news. It's Manya. Some kind of accident. The hospital called. They wouldn't tell us anything. Do you have the kids? No? I'm going to your house. Call your neighbor to see if the kids are at home. The kids are in school except Toto? Where's Toto? At your house? Shit. The EMTs must not have known he was there. You think maybe he was napping. Look, tell your neighbor to go over and stay with Toto. I'll get the kids. Where's their school? Don't worry. Okay? You go to the hospital. Field's on his way. I'll meet you there with all three kids. Don't worry."

Normally, it takes nearly an hour and a half to get to Daniel's place in Lawrence. I didn't want to get a ticket. I didn't want to get in a wreck. I tried everybody from my cell while I was driving. I called Daniel's house to tell the neighbor I was on my way. Thank God, she was there. Toto was there with her, and he was fine. Where was everybody else?

So this is what they went through with me after the tractor accident. What a nightmare—not knowing anything.

Deal. I'd have to see him. Not thinking about that right now. How to get to Daniel's kids as fast as possible? Safely.

How to help them and Daniel? If Manya is really hurt, Daniel will be devastated. Devastated is not a big enough word. He is almost like a little boy around Manya. He *is* a little boy around her. She doesn't have three kids. She has four kids.

The drive passed in a blur, me leaning forward over the steering wheel the entire way, on high alert. Thank goodness the roads were free of snow and ice.

I relieved the neighbor, Mrs. Carson, thanked her, and asked her for more details on how to get to Ivan's and Danny's schools. I jiggled Toto and hunted for a bottle for him. Mrs. Carson explained that he used a cup. She handed me some snacks for the kids. I found the diaper bag and Manya's purse. Still limping a bit, I looked around the kitchen and briefly wandered through the house to see whether some object might jog my poor mind. It was racing but very sluggish, all at the same time. There was blood all over the bathroom floor. And some kind of packaging and an information sheet. I tried Mom again at work. "Mom, it's Wally. Mom, something's happened to Manya. Better get to the hospital in Lawrence, okay? I've got Toto, and I'm going to get Ivan and Danny. I'll meet you there. Daniel and Field are on their way. Can you call everyone else? I've been trying for over an hour." Ah, a car seat or two. "Mrs. Carson, does Danny still use a car seat?"

The scene at the hospital was pandemonium, mostly because Daniel was wailing and wild. He struggled with two security guards who attempted to restrain him. I knew instantly that Manya must be dead. Daniel tried to wrench himself free as I walked in with the boys. Field grabbed his shoulders. "Daniel," Danny ran to him. Miraculously, Daniel calmed himself. It was drastic. One second, he was screaming and looking like he might punch the guard if he could get his hand free, and the next second, he was perfectly sedate.

I tell you what. The power of that transformation made me want to have kids. Here was a man, my too sweet, too rational brother, made completely insane by grief and then made instantly sane by overwhelming love. I knew I would never be quite the same after that moment.

When Deal got there, he took over in a quiet, natural way. He dealt with the authorities, medical and legal. He delegated jobs: one of us to call the funeral home; one of us to take note of the medication Manya had apparently used and the circumstances around her death, as we knew them; one of us to get death certificates.

Field hovered over Daniel. Mama and I played with Daniel's kids and struggled to answer their questions. We soft-pedaled our responses, hoping to let them down slowly. Alicia watched her kids. Anna fetched items as needed. Before we left, Daniel took the older boys outside to talk. When they returned, everybody took turns hugging them.

So this is my family, pulled apart in adversity, pulling together in adversity. Dawn? Dawn did not belong here anymore. Who had she been? A figment of my imagination? A figment of my insecurity? She seemed to have been in my world a long, long time ago. She would have been more real to me had she died. The people who are real are the people who come around when life gets crunchy or slick. Or when life gets really drab. Olive drab or just plain grainy gray. Dawn had been someone to take to a party. A flicker of candlelight. A spray of champagne. Someone who dotted her i's with a heart. What was that note with her handwriting on it? I'll look at it later. I need to be with my family now.

Chapter 34

ANNA

Deal left in the spring when the crows were cawing. Manya died in winter. The crows were still cawing.

Manya's service was small and bittersweet. Her remaining family had been contacted but could not afford to make the long journey.

In the doorway of the unimpressive storefront church, I heard Wally ask Field, "What the hell, man. Were you poppin' her too?"

"Are you crazy, Wally?" Field asked, and I saw Wally pull some kind of note out of his pocket.

I shushed Wally and pulled on his elbow to lead him into the church, but he jerked away from me.

"I found this note in your desk, Field." He waved the note in Field's face. "You told me to look for the B&T papers the day Manya died, remember. Well, I found the papers, and I found this note in your desk drawer. This note is from Dawn, and she's thanking you for your visit and asking you to come over again some time. What the fuck?"

"You're crazy, man," Field said. "I fixed your sink that time you were in Topeka taking your CPA exam. Water everywhere. You knew about that."

"So...why was she asking you to come back?"

"How the hell do I know? Maybe she wanted us all to come visit. Maybe she wanted to play with the kids."

"Well, why'd you keep the note in your drawer at work then, huh, if you're so goddamned innocent?"

"I don't know, man. She sent a note. I stuck it in my drawer. I forgot about it. You got to quit looking for enemies, bro."

"Fuck you, Field," Wally said as Jonah entered the church.

"Not now," she said. She looked from one to the other.

"You take the cake, Wally," Field said. "After all I've done for you." He mouthed, "Asshole," silently so Jonah wouldn't hear and went to join his family.

JONAH

A priest conducted the funeral in the Russian Orthodox tradition of Manya's childhood. He was very kind. Before we started, he showed all the kids how to make the sign of the cross, the special Orthodox way. "You put your thumb and your first two fingers together to signify the Trinity," he said. "You put your last two fingers together to signify the duality, the human and divine natures of Jesus. You bend the last two fingers down against your palm to represent the unity of the human and divine in Christ. When you make the sign of the cross, the whole dogma is in your hand."

The kids may not have understood what dogma is, but they loved trying to get their fingers in the correct position.

"Is this right?" Danny asked the young priest while tugging on his robe. Ivan, Marguerite, and Allen practiced crossing themselves right to left and nudging me to look. I nodded and smiled to show them I saw and to acknowledge they were doing it perfectly.

Gilded pictures of Jesus, Mary, and the disciples warred with the secondhand sofas and mismatched rug fragments in the makeshift chapel. The priest wore a black cassock, a white chasuble, and a white stole with gold trim and gold cross designs. A large cross hung down to his chest. He wore a funny black hat that looked like a costume for a mushroom.

When the service began, the boys stopped practicing crossing themselves. They looked stiff and brave. I held Danny's hand. He sat between Daniel and me. Ivan was on the other side of Daniel next to Wally. Both of the boys were dressed in jackets and ties.

Anna was holding Toto on her lap. He was, mercifully, asleep. Deal reached for my hand, tears streaming down his face.

In the candelabra light, the priest swung frankincense in a censer at the foot of the coffin as the choir chanted in eerie harmonies that were strangely soothing. The burning of the incense, the burning of the many candles, like the burning of our fields—what was it all for if not resurrection?

When my family stood to sing, the trunk of each person's body seemed to shrink in on itself. Even though to outsiders, they might seem to be standing tall, I saw their boughs laden with the wet, heavy snow of grief and misfortune.

ANNA

After the service, I took the kids back to Daniel's so they wouldn't see Manya lowered into the ground. The rest of the crew faithfully trooped to the frozen cemetery in their motley cortege of cars.

"What does it mean 'die,' Aunt Anna?" Danny asked me.

"It means Mama is gone to Heaven, stupid," Ivan told him.

"Ivan, don't be mean to your brother. He hasn't had time yet to learn as many things as you."

"I'm sorry, Aunt Anna. I don't want Mama to be in Heaven. I want her to be home with us."

"Me too," Danny said. "Why don't we go to Heaven and get her to come home now?" He started to cry.

"You can't go to Heaven 'til you're dead," Ivan yelled at him.

"Hush, Ivan," I said. "You're scaring him."

"Then how do I get dead?" Danny asked smearing his tears across his little face. "I'll get dead and go to Heaven and bring Mama home," he said brightly.

"No, honey, it doesn't work that way. Once you die, you can't come back. But you know what? Your Mama loves you so much. She didn't want to leave you. She couldn't help it. And her love lives with you in your heart and never goes away. Can you feel her love, sweetheart?"

Danny nodded seriously. "I still want her here. I want her to make me some cereal with a banana in it right now." He stomped his foot. "I want her to take Ivan to school and give Toto a nap and come and play with *me*. We haven't finished our castle we were making. I want to make my castle."

"That stupid castle," Ivan said. "I already knocked it down."

JONAH

Daniel, after his moments of violent despair in the hospital, returned to the salve of routine. He was close to finishing the semester, both the courses he was taking and those he was teaching. He didn't want to take or give incompletes because that would put him behind next semester. I moved into Ivan's room, and Ivan moved in with his brothers so I could help manage the household for now. Daniel buried himself in his makeshift office in his bedroom while I shopped for groceries or ran a carpool for Ivan and Danny. I put the word out for a part-time nanny so I could return to the bank in January. The others didn't live in Lawrence, but they came often to visit or help out. We planned a simple Christmas, unsure if Wally and Deal would both come.

Although by nature a sound sleeper, I frequently heard muffled cries from Daniel's room. Once I got up the nerve to knock lightly and go in. Daniel's despair had not diminished in intensity, just in volume, so he wouldn't wake the rest of us. I sat on the edge of his bed and rubbed his back for a long time. I got a cool washcloth to wipe his face and eyes. "She loved you all so much," I said over and over. "She didn't mean to leave you."

Ivan became more and more wretched with his siblings and had to be put in time out repeatedly for breaking a toy or even a household object. He devised a game in which he hid Danny's blankie or Danny's favorite stuffed bunny. He only told Danny where he put it if Danny performed some service for him, like making his bed or cleaning up his toys. It was a good thing his school would soon be on Christmas break. We were already getting notes from his teacher. Danny retreated into himself. He was sweet as always, but his sparkle was dimmed, temporarily I hoped. Toto's stomach was sour for a while. Periodically, he whimpered in a halting way, no matter whether he'd eaten or been changed or napped.

Field, because of his recent experience with the lawsuit still pending against his firm, was in charge of legal action against the Internet company that had sold Manya the home abortion kit. Wally, though, had a lot more time on his hands, and, in practice, he was the one who consulted with attorneys and physicians and the FDA. He moved back into his own house.

Did anyone famous say something about recovery being the business of living? If not, they should have. Even before I recover from winter, I get ready to order seeds for the spring garden. Before I recover from putting peas and greens in the ground, I'm getting ready to sow beans. I don't know that my back has ever quite recovered from seasons of hoeing, and then it's time to recover from the mists of canning. I find my recovery time has been taking longer and longer, and my to-do lists have been getting shorter and shorter. After all, I don't need to feed six any more. I have to recover from feeding six and learn what it's like to feed just one.

I decided to call Wally to find out whether he'd come over Christmas Day if Deal was here. Then I wondered, why on earth would we invite Deal over? I don't really want him around. I pictured the house with just me and the kids and the grandkids, and there was definitely much joy and rambunctiousness, but there was also definitely a hole where Deal should be, not to speak of Manya, God bless her. I didn't want any more holes. I could feel the pall that hole would cast if he weren't there.

Then I pictured us all together. Awkwardness. Some people keeping their distance from Deal, busying themselves playing with the kids and their new toys. But no palls, no holes other than Manya, which was a hole no one could fill. I decided to give something to the less fortunate in her memory. She would have appreciated that. Maybe some less fortunate Russians. Surely, there'd be plenty of those.

"Wally," I reached his machine, "it's Mama. Call me back when you get a chance. I need to check out something with you. I love you, honey."

"Field," I called him after I got off the phone with Wally's machine. "How are you? What's happening with your lawsuit? Has Wally learned any more about Manya?"

"Mine's on hold 'til January," Field said. "On Manya…Wally's found out plenty. He and I have hired a lawyer. We haven't told Daniel yet. We're afraid he won't want to prosecute."

"Listen," I said, "would you mind calling Wally? I want to find out whether he'll come home for Christmas if Deal is here. Do you think it's a bad idea? Having Deal here? I called Wally and left a message, but I thought maybe he'd tell me what he thought I wanted to hear. He might tell you the truth."

"Really, Mama, it's up to you and Wally," Field said. "I'll call him if you want. The rest of us will be fine with whatever."

Sometimes, I got impatient with Field's diplomacy. Lack of interest really. Too much like Deal. On the other hand, maybe some of Field's noncommittal style came from me always wanting to please. All right then, forget it. I'm not checking with Wally. I don't want Deal around yet. Maybe tomorrow. Maybe never. I'm *not* inviting him for Christmas Day. So there.

When my sweet mother, Anna, was pregnant with me, she told me she felt huge. She felt she carried all the seas of time within her and, of course, in a way she did. You know, when I was in high school, they used to say these words that always stuck in my head: "ontogeny recapitulates phylogeny," that the development of the embryo proceeds apace in each pregnant woman in a manner similar to the evolution of species. I don't think they still believe that so much.

According to scientists now, our diversity of species began as a puff of smoke, an idea of love in the mind of the world represented by atoms like nitrogen, hydrogen, and oxygen. If you swirl these elements in a lab, and maybe some others, you can create the building blocks of life. They've done it. I read about it in *Newsweek*.

From then on, it's only a matter of millions of years before the bit of organic molecule becomes an amoeba, then a fish, then a land creature with four legs, and, eventually, a land creature that has two of its four legs become arms. The Christian God managed this span of development in seven days. A woman manages creation in nine months.

My mother supposedly felt huge when she was pregnant with me. She felt like a whale, she said. When I emerged from the belly of the whale, she named me Jonah even though I turned out to be a girl. Since I did turn out to be a girl, I was never quite sure her feeling of hugeness was a compliment to me. Maybe my reticence in life has come, in part, to prove to people that I am not obnoxiously large, that I won't run over them like a whale person might.

I didn't have that huge feeling when I was pregnant with my five kids. I'm a small person, 5'2", and the babies growing inside were more like teeny critters in a possum's pouch. I felt like a baby carrier and not really like a human. More like an animal. I didn't feel I had a personal identity any more. I had an important function, to be sure, to keep the fetus from getting bumped, to eat well, and to take my vitamins so the fetus could grow up to be a fine specimen. But the me I had known all my life wandered away. I guess she felt shoved aside and didn't like it. She *was* shoved aside. Once the kids were born, they became huge for me. When the kids got older, and I had more time, I couldn't find that old version of me any more. Honestly, I didn't really know where to look. Then the grandkids came.

Now, though, I'm developing more hugeness. I swell up not to be taken over. When I don't remember to inflate, I feel I am just a pawn in my children's game plans. They have these strong ideas about who I should be. If I don't become a whale person, they just invent me. At this late date, I have finally started inventing myself.

I feel a swelling in my belly as it greets the day. You know some people just don't get trounced. They don't deflate. If the day knocks on them, they resonate. If the day pricks them, they patch the hole. If the day allows, they bounce. That's the new me. I'm one of those big plastic balls with the bright colored panels the kids bat around in a swimming pool. I'm going to have surgery on my eyelids and throw my shoulders back and go "Harrumph," a lot. The other day, I was reading about the trials and tribulations of Jennifer Aniston in the checkout line when a woman cut in front of me. "Hold on, Madam," I said. I looked at her without blinking. "Excuse me, but I was here first."

ANNA

Alicia and her kids and I drove up to Lawrence to bake Christmas cookies with Daniel's brood. The kids cut Christmas trees and stars and bells and candy canes out of dough and decorated the shapes with colored sprinkles and crushed peppermints and confectioner's sugar mixed with food coloring. We had quite a variety of realistic and, well, not so realistic, designs.

Mama sat at the dinette table and mended ancient Christmas stockings.

"How are you, girls?" Mama stopped sewing for a minute and looked up at us.

"I'm okay, Jonah," Alicia said. "We're doing okay."

"What about you, Anna?" Mama asked. She finished stitching sequins around the toe of Wally's green felt stocking to hide the threadbare places. His name was cross-stitched across the top in red: "Wallace."

"When did you make this stocking, Mama?" I asked coming over.

"Before you were born, dear," she said, looking off into space. "How old is Wally now, 29? Probably for his first Christmas." Her beautiful blue eyes, a little paler and more heavy-lidded than I remembered, filled. She laid down Wally's stocking and picked up the next one in the pile. I saw Manya's name written on it, and I groaned.

Mama looked at me, then down at the stocking.

"We've all been through so much lately." She patted my arm. "Funny thing, though," she smiled, "when Manya left us, Wally returned. I'd been doing pretty good, considering, and when Wally moved in, it felt like they put one of those tents over our house like they do when they spray for termites. Only they forgot to take the tent off after they sprayed. I couldn't get out from under that tent no matter what. I went to the Barnes & Noble in Wichita and listened to CD's. I picked out about ten rollicking ones and some comedy tapes too. I played them really loud to try to pull Wally out of his funk. I think it probably drove him crazy, but it never helped lift the tent off. I tried heart-to-heart talks. Nothing. The only thing that seemed to help was when Alicia or Manya brought the kids over. Then Wally would play. Or when you came over, Anna, and danced for him. For a little while, he'd be okay."

"What a nightmare, Mama." I rubbed her shoulder.

"It was. It was."

"But what about before Wally moved in?" Alicia stopped transferring unbaked cookies to a cookie sheet and moved closer to Jonah. "How did you manage after Deal left?"

"I don't know, Alicia," she said. "I guess I don't want to talk about it right now. The hardest part was for me to see Wally hurting so bad that the tent came down over the house and stayed there."

Chapter 35

WALLY

Field and I took off the Thursday before Christmas Eve to get Daniel out of the house. Field and I had agreed to stay away from emotional topics like Deal and Dawn. We didn't want to add any more hurt to Daniel's plate of suffering.

Mom, Anna, and Alicia were going to take the five kids to see Santa.

Originally, we'd planned to get up early in hopes of seeing wildlife along the north shore of Clinton Lake, but it was ten o'clock by the time we started walking. We hoped we still might catch a glimpse of gray fox or coyote at dusk on the way back.

It was a clear and beautiful day, the sky so blue it can move you into what I call the blue sky zone.

"Daniel, do you know what I mean when I say blue sky zone?" I asked.

"Blue sky zone?" he repeated.

"Yeah. You know when you wake up kind of grumpy because you got the wrong size underwear, and you have to go back to the store and exchange it, and there's going to be mobs of people and no place to park, and you step outside, and Boom, you know you're not going to the store today, you're going to do everything you can to just feel the sun and see as much of that sky as you possibly can before you die?"

"Yeah," he said, "I think I know what you mean. It's like when a waterfall takes you away in the thunder of it. In the cascade of it. You get mesmerized, and your troubles disappear for a little while."

"Yeah," I said peering through the woods that surrounded us and trying to catch a glimpse of the lake. "Mesmerized. By nature."

"Or sex," Field said, slowing his pace a bit to get in on the conversation.

"Sex is not a blue sky zone," I said. "Sex is a red zone."

"Hot potato zone," Field said.

"New potato," Daniel said. "Fresh every time."

"Nope," Field said. "Hot potato. You stick with your new potatoes. I'll stick with my hot potatoes. Speaking of which, Wally, I don't think Deal ever had sex with Dawn."

Conversation stopped. Hiking stopped. We were walking by a beaver dam, and I pretended to examine it. It looked like any other beaver dam. "For Christ's sake, Field," I said. "We're hiking about ten whole minutes, and here we are talking about sex. Plus, you're bringing up a taboo subject, you know that, you idiot. I thought we agreed—"

"—Oh, come off it, Wally. It's not a secret any more that she left. She left. She was the idiot. I'm sorry, but it takes two to tango, and she left. Nobody made her. He didn't make her."

"You saying I couldn't keep her?"

"I'm saying she left. You, little brother, are a wonderful guy. You work hard. You have a big heart. You like making columns of numbers line up nice and straight." He laughed. "You want the best for everybody. Some women would knock themselves out to make you happy. You just didn't pick one of those. You picked someone with a lot of flash. Flash in the pan."

"Watch out, Field, you're talking about my wife."

"She's not your wife any more, Wally, and you know it," he continued. "I'm just trying to make you feel better. Alicia was visiting with Anna the other day. I think Deal dropped in on Anna at work, and they talked. I don't know. Women." Field grunted. "But Alicia got the very strong impression that Deal never slept with Dawn."

"Well then, why the fuck did she move in with him? Why the fuck did he allow it? Why did he tear our family apart?" I kicked the dirt, but my toe must have hit a rock. I could feel it through my hiking boots.

"Beats me, Wally," Field said. "Too much higher math for me. You're the accountant. I'm just the construction worker. By the way, I've been wanting to ask you: what were you doing out on Dad's tractor that night?"

"By the way," I retorted. "I've been wanting to ask *you*: what were you doing with that note from Dawn in your desk for what, six months…a year?"

Daniel had been stripping the bark from the handle of a walking stick. Now he pointed the walking stick at us. "Enough, you guys," he said. "Put you guys together for five minutes and listen to you. Brothers, remember? We're brothers. This is not the Olympic Games. This is not the Roman Coliseum.

"Come on. Back to the blue sky zone. Look, there's a bluebird. Goddamn, Manya loved a bluebird. She was a regular bluebird freak. Whenever she saw a bluebird, she would cross herself, and bow her head for a minute. You know when Catholics do that, don't you wish you could do that? Like they have this talisman they don't have to carry around. No rabbit's foot or anything. Just cross yourself, and God is on your side. Pretty neat trick. Almost made me want to convert."

"You?" Field and I shouted at the same time and burst out laughing.

"Oh, shut up, what do you know?" Daniel asked, still perfecting that walking stick handle with his penknife.

"I know I love you guys," Field said. "That's all I know, and all I need to know. Truce, Wally."

During our lunch break, we skipped stones to see whose could go the farthest or skip the most times. Believe it or not, Daniel could skip a stone close to fifteen times although Field's arm was strongest and his stones went farther. In the afternoon, we hiked on through the hardwood forest and almost made it to the end of the trail.

"We'd better turn back so we don't run out of daylight," Daniel said. "Come on, guys. I've got to get home."

We didn't realize that the moon would be almost full. As soon as the sun set, there it was, this gigantic orb, the way it is in a children's book, resting on the earth and glowing through the stark outlines of soaring shagbark hickories. As the moon rose, its eerie light turned the lake silver, and its image echoed in all the ripples of the lake.

Field gave a slow whistle. "I got to take the kids out more."

"Man," Daniel said inhaling, "me too."

"Time for me to get some kids *to* take out more," I said, and we all laughed.

"Good idea though," Field said softly. "Hang on to that thought."

DANIEL

I think of my Manya, my bluebird, every day. When I'm cleaning up the kitchen, she's there with me. When I make my bed in the morning, she says, "Daniel, *moy daragoy*, you are so a good man. Look at you. You making bed nice for sleeping. In Russia, man is not making bed. Man is complaining how woman making bed. You so a fine man, moy daragoy."

I can almost feel her hugging me, and I sit down on the partially made bed and cry. I look up to check that no small child is standing in the doorway watching. Then I gently close the door, but the tears have gone. So I stand up and survey the room and hold her photo close to my chest and hug her back. My Manya, my bluebird of happiness.

You're not supposed to lean on your kids emotionally. You're supposed to be the Dad. When times are tough, you're still supposed to be the Dad.

I am so grateful to Mama for moving in and helping out. I could not have done it without her. I mean, how the hell, can anyone manage three kids without help? My hat's off to those single mothers in poverty that seem to be everywhere you look. Maybe some day, I can help one of them.

Right now, just putting one foot in front of the other is the best I can manage. Ivan's been having some trouble. His trouble is loud. It's out there, really obvious. Danny's the one I worry about most. His trouble is soft. It could be overlooked if I weren't super careful.

I hug them a lot. I try to spend time with each of them, but, my God, just working and grocery shopping is almost more than I can bear.

When I drive from here to there, I see Manya everywhere. Calling, calling. She's always calling. She's trying all these phone numbers, and no one answers. I want to tell her to stop calling. "Manya, milaya, you can stop calling now. It's finished now. No more calling." But she doesn't listen. She keeps calling. She calls in Russian, and no one can understand her. I can catch a word here and there.

I miss her terribly. Her hugs were…what can I say? Her hugs were like you were in a nest. Sweet straw. Always April. Bereft means you take away the strength of the hug. You take away its protection. Then you take away the person who was hugging. You take away your own strength. You walk around as a pair of pants and a shirt. Then you put this violently hurting spot that consumes you underneath the shirt. That's what bereft means. How the hell am I supposed to be a Dad as a pair of pants?

"The Lord works in mysterious ways," they say. "He doesn't give you more than you can bear." Who made up all that garbage? The Lord takes away and leaves you with air. And if you have kids, you're stuck with air. You can't puncture your lungs, the way you'd like to, because you have to keep going for the kids' sake. You have to keep breathing in and out, in and out, in and out, 86,400 times a day, sometimes more, and that's just in one day. The days stretch out interminably, and this is supposed to be the time when I relish watching my young sons growing and learning. Well, there's relish in the fridge. I'm not sure how long it will keep.

I've been struggling to finish my dissertation so I can start making more money for my boys. "Prairie Fire," my dissertation is called. "A history of prairie fires in southeast Kansas: communities in the making." I had a lot of trouble getting it approved by my committee at KU. The dissertation is a good distraction. Surprising that I'm able to make any headway on it at all. The topic inspires me. Lots of forward motion so long as it doesn't get out of control. Sort of like the prairie fires I'm writing about.

Prairie fires are the lifeblood of the Flint Hills. There are two kinds: the kind that God or an arsonist sets and the kind deliberately set by the farmer, or more likely, the rancher. We white folk picked up the skill from the Native American, the Osage and the Kaw who used to live hereabouts. The Indians observed that the buffalo—and the elk and the deer—which also lived here, were better nourished when lightning struck. Fire could burn the woody plants from their grazing grounds, and the bluestem grasses, on which the buffalo fed and on which our cattle fatten today, could thrive. The Indians began setting intentional prairie fires in early spring as we still do today.

When we were little, Deal used to let us stay up to watch the prairie burn. Of course, you have to wait 'til there's moisture in the air, forty to seventy per cent, in fact. If conditions are too dry, you're not permitted to set a fire. And you have to make sure there's a firebreak between the area to be burned and any dwellings or livestock. Plenty of neighbors come to help out.

One time, the four of us kids were at the edge of the field that would be burned. It was dark and cloudy. You couldn't see many stars. We were hyper, very excited. Wally kept pulling my hair, and Field came over and said, "Cut it out, Wally," and picked him up and moved him away from me. I remember it because Field didn't usually pay attention to me that much. I think Mama had left him in charge while she got food for the neighbors. Wally started running out in the direction of where the fire would be set. He was looking at Field to see if Field was noticing, then running back. Wally was just hassling Field to keep his attention. He didn't like that Field had been able to pick him up as if he were a chair. Young as I was, I was worried Wally would get burned, and I started to cry. Anna punched me in the face. "Toughen up," she said.

Then, whoosh, the fire was set. We watched a row of flame, maybe as long as five football fields, engulf the ten-acre pasture. Fire rumbled across the land. It crackled at first, then roared like a train blasting its way down the track. Smoke swirled upward. Flames licked the dark of the sky away with blazing hues of orange, red and yellow. A breeze created whirling dervishes of fire.

As a child, I wondered how come grown-ups were allowed to create such a conflagration. I would have been reprimanded had I even lit a match to watch it glow. Of course, I'd been told over and over again how very dangerous it was to start a prairie fire without the county's permission. When God set lightning down on a parched land, people lost their crops, their livestock, their homes, and sometimes their lives.

After Deal and our neighbors set the prairie fire, the land was ashes, and we all smelled like smoke. Mama fed the neighbors and made us take a bath. She fixed us some cocoa before we brushed our teeth.

Fire and controlled devastation. Purification and resurrection. Neighbors helping neighbors. Clean hair and cocoa. That's what my dissertation is all about.

Chapter 36

ANNA

Milam called me the other day. He sounded kind of distraught.

"Anna, hey babe, listen, don't hang up. I can't stop thinking about you. I hardly got a chance to know you, and all that stuff happened. Did you get the card I sent? And the flowers for your sister-in-law? How's your brother? He's okay, right?"

"Yeah, hey Milam. It's been a while. I've been kind of out of commission. Harsh times in my family, you might say. Crows coming home to roost."

"You mean chickens, right?"

"Crows. Chickens. Whatever."

"So how are you doing?"

"I'm okay, I guess. I'm probably going to move to Lawrence after Christmas to help my brother Daniel out. Mom's going to move back to the farm and start her job back. But I can waitress anywhere. And I can still go to KC to take class."

"Oh. If you move to Lawrence, I'll never get to see you."

"You can if you want to. You don't have to work on the weekends, right? You know what, I don't even know where you work. What you do. That's crazy."

"It is crazy. Here I meet someone I want to get to know, and I don't know what you do either. I work construction. And I go to school at night. I'm thinking architecture. Get those prereqs out of the way. So, no, I don't usually have to work weekends."

"Well, see? You can come up if you want. Hang out with the kids."

"Oh, great."

"You don't like kids?"

"I love kids, but—"

"—Well, we'd have time alone too. We could make time alone. Not that much privacy up there, but—"

"—Anna, how about tonight? Want to go eat?"

"I've got to work."

"Tomorrow night?"

"I've got to work."

"Anna, are you blowing me off?"

"I guess we should talk some time."

"Oh, man. When a woman says, 'we should talk,' it is not usually a good sign."

"True. Not usually. Look, what are you doing for Christmas? Want to come out to the farm and hang out? Everyone but Deal will be there, probably. That's usually a good sign, right? When a woman invites you home to meet the fam?"

"That's usually a very good sign. I could come out after we open presents at my folks."

"Okay, then. Come on out."

JONAH

Christmas without Deal turned out better than I had dared to hope.

In preparation for the family's descent, I aired out the upstairs rooms and left their doors ajar so the heat from our cranky system would reach them again. Bring them back into the fold. Everyone showed up Christmas Eve except Anna who had to work.

Wally took the kids to pick out a tree. He dug the boxes of Christmas ornaments out of the shed and adjusted the tree in its stand while Alicia and I instructed him on which direction looked straight. Seems sometimes like us women would even like to tell a guy which direction is up too, doesn't it?

I put an ornament on here and there, but mostly I sat and took it all in as everyone went through the boxes, struggled with the strings of lights that drive us crazy every year, and placed each beloved ornament one more time. I made them some hot chocolate. We had Christmas music on. When Anna arrived Christmas morning, she let me kiss her cheeks, cold and sparkling with winter. They let her put the star on top.

Everyone brought gifts and special dishes and their best behavior. Every time I wondered how Deal was faring, I was distracted by the morning chaos of stockings and wrapping paper and kids expanding to fill all available space.

Before lunch, I moved other family photos to one side, and we all gathered around a photograph of Manya on the mantel. The priest from Manya's church had given Daniel an ornate gold candlestick and a blessed candle. "The priest told me a candle is a prayer without words," Daniel said as he lit it. Everyone nodded as if they understood. Each of us took a turn placing an item on the makeshift altar, the little ones climbing onto a stool to do so. Daniel brought a painting of a bluebird. Little Danny approached the painting, turned to us scowling and yelled, "Stop looking at me." We pretended to avert our eyes. He quickly kissed the bluebird painting, placed one of his toy blocks on the mantel, jumped down, and ran behind Daniel to hide.

In the afternoon, Hollis' son, Milam, joined us at Anna's invitation. He roughhoused with the kids and played with them with their new toys. Occasionally, I saw him glance at Anna and grin. He offered to drive her to work after supper, but she said she had her car. Although Milam was built more like Field, his grin was so boyish, so heartfelt, it reminded me of Wally long ago. I found myself giving him a bear hug. "Thank you so much for joining us." He hugged me back, like Manya would have. "Thank you so much for having me," he said.

DEAL

"Best piece of ass I ever had."

"That right?" asked the man on the barstool next to me.

"Yup."

"I remember when I was ranching out in Comanche County," the stranger said, "there was a girl I saw in a bar one night. Hair black as jet. Teeth white as the clouds floating across a prairie moon. Lovely thing. She followed me home in her car. Can't see why she wanted to do that. Lonely, I expect. I'll treasure that memory though. Don't matter the reason. I expect you feel the same way."

"What? What are you talking about?" I asked.

"Now, don't go getting all riled up. I thought you told me that girl you had home with you was a juicy fruit treat," the stranger said.

"Juicy fruit treat, is that right?" someone asked. Familiar voice. I turned. Anna.

"An…Anna, what on earth are you doing here?"

"I could ask you the same, Deal," Anna said. "I work here. What on earth are you doing here? And who's the juicy fruit treat? Who's the best piece of ass? Huh, Deal? You can tell me, right? We're best buds, huh, Deal, aren't we?"

"Hey, it's Christmas. I thought I could get a drink here. Celebrate. I didn't think anyone I knew would come in here. Everyone's at the farm but me, right?"

"Feeling sorry for yourself, Deal? Need a little anonymity for your sins, huh?"

I got to my feet, pushed away from the bar, and staggered to the door.

"There goes my daddy," Anna said to the stranger.

"Pleasure to meet him," the stranger said.

ANNA

The next morning, I started calling around 5 a.m. The phone rang and rang. Deal must be hung over. Surely, he wouldn't have left for the farm at this hour.

Finally, he picked up. "Who is it?" he said. "Go back to sleep, whoever you are. It's too early," and he hung up the phone.

I just called back again, but he didn't answer.

I hopped in my car and drove over to his apartment. First time I'd been there in all these months. I was a little nervous, but mostly, I was ready for bear. I banged on the flimsy screen door and held my finger on the doorbell. I was getting ready to take off my shoe and bang louder when Deal opened the door, a robe pulled around him. "Anna," he said. "Oh, honey, give me a break. Just give me a chance to wake up a little. Why don't you come back in an hour or so. I'll take you out to breakfast."

"Damn it, Deal," I said. "Go get in the shower. I'll sit in your living room and wait. You fuckin' goddamn ought to be ashamed of yourself."

"I am. That I am," he said turning away.

"You got a girl in there?" I asked.

"Come on, Anna. Give me a break."

Deal came out clean, hair wet, holding two mugs of steaming coffee.

"Any milk?" I asked. "Any sugar?"

"Sorry," he said. "If I'd known you were coming. Maybe there's some sugar in there. Hold on."

He came back with a bag of sugar and a spoon. "No milk," he said. "Fake stuff."

I shook my head.

"What on earth is wrong with you, Deal? What were you doing in a bar talking to a stranger about your private business? Being drunk?"

"What can I say?" Deal said shrugging. "What is there to say any more?"

"Deal," I said setting my coffee down and kneeling by his chair. "It's your daughter. We used to care about each other, remember?"

Deal just shook his head. "That was a long time ago," he said.

"Goddamn it," I said. "I'm not going to let you turn into someone else. I thought you and Dawn were never a couple. Last night, she was the best piece of ass you ever had. Or I guess that was Dawn. Maybe there've been lots of Dawns we don't know about, never knew about. Who the fuck were you talking about last night?"

"Let's see," Deal began.

“Oh my God,” I said. “Let’s see?”

“Yes, I was talking about Dawn,” Deal said. “Or the alcohol was talking. Isn’t that what they say? It wasn’t me; it was the alcohol talking.” He grunted.

“So you *were* a couple? All this time, you’ve been putting it out there that you weren’t, but you really were?”

The phone rang, and Deal went into the kitchen to get it.

“Wrong number,” he said, returning with the coffee pot and offering to fill my cup. “Now where were we?” he asked.

“Dawn,” I said.

“Dawn,” he said. “I seem to remember a Dawn. Look, Anna,” he said. “You’re my daughter. I can’t talk to you about this stuff.”

”But you can talk to a perfect stranger in a bar?”

“What were you doing there anyway?” he asked.

“I told you. I work there. I’ve been working there. Nobody knows about it because Strayhorns don’t go to bars, right? Hah! I can’t make jack shit working at that café. People around here may not go to cafés. But, believe it or not, they go to bars. A lot. And not just students either. You’re not the only one that has troubles and no one but strangers to tell them to.”

“Everybody in this family has a trouble, and no one to tell it to,” Deal said. “Wonder what Jonah’s secret is? Wonder what Daniel’s secret is or Field’s? Or Alicia’s? My secret is this. My secret is…I feel like giving up. How about you take off now, honey. Please don’t take offense. Just let me go back to bed for a change. Let somebody else feed the livestock. Let somebody else get out of bed and lubricate the tractor. Let somebody else clean up the mess in the shed.”

Chapter 37

WALLY

I'd been fixing up my place since moving back from Mama's. Very satisfying. I'd always wanted a paneled den. A place you could put your feet up, invite some people over, have a couple of beers. Maybe watch a movie or a game. I pictured some brown leather overstuffed chairs, like in a lawyer's office, and a sofa with deep cushions. Someplace that was hard to get out of so people would stay longer.

I started going to a young adults group at church, and every now and then, although she was Catholic, Amanda and I went out. She was the night nurse who took care of me when I was in the SICU. She looked like a younger version of Mama, but she was more…animated. Not that Mama isn't. But, Mama had been awful somber lately. Come to think of it, damn, I was a selfish SOB. I hadn't even thought how much Mama might be suffering. I wondered if she was. She had to be.

When I was a little boy, I loved my Mama so, so much. Field and Mama, they were my world. If I was home and they were home, everything was all right in the universe of my house. Wonder whether Deal ever felt that I shut him out? I was always so certain he shut me out. Oh boy. Nothing good ever comes from speculation and introspection except complication and confusion. How the hell does anybody ever know who did what to whom in their family if they consider changing their mind about family history when they grow up?

Anyway, Amanda's fun. Bubbly and kind of cherubic. I'm just glad when I see her that I'm not in the SICU. My cast will be coming off soon, and you'd have to know to look, to see my limp. I'm actually grateful to be alive, but I think I owe Deal some money for that tractor.

DEAL

So much has happened, I've stopped worrying about what people think of me. Well, that's not completely true. God knows, I'll never be a saint. But, truly, for now, my kids are more important to me than me. My beautiful Daniel with no church in him to speak of is more saintly than most. How he can bear up under this loss is a mystery to me. I guess he goes on because of the kids.

My ornery Wally. He's been such a trooper, working on Manya's case, driving up to Lawrence after all day at the office to give Daniel a break or shop or whatever's needed. Field, so much like me in so many ways. Good to his family. My Jonah or who used to be *my* Jonah. Aloof but reasonably friendly on the surface. Wish I could summon up the nerve to call Wally. I've got to fortify myself and do it.

The phone rang. Believe it or not, it was Wally.

"Deal," he said, "it's Wally."

"Hi, son. How are you? Actually, I was just going to call you."

"Deal," he said again, "I think I owe you for the tractor repairs. They must have cost a bundle. I *know* I owe you."

"Son, if me paying for fixing that tractor could fix any part of the rift between us, I'd pay for those repairs a hundred times over. Well..." I tried to make a joke. "I don't know if I could afford a hundred."

"Deal, meet me at my house in half an hour."

"What? Okay, son. Half an hour. Whatever you say."

Seeing Wally in the house we helped him buy when he married Dawn was about as high on my top ten list of things to do before I died as having a tractor roll on me. But if he wanted me at his house, hey, that's where I'd go.

It didn't take a full half hour to get there, even driving as slow as I would let myself get by with. He was waiting on the front porch, though it was cold enough to see your breath steam. He had on one of those Mr. Rogers' type of sweaters. I never could wear those.

He led me into a den I couldn't remember ever seeing before.

"Have you fixed this up?" I asked.

"Yeah, this is all new here lately," Wally said. "Can I get you anything?"

"I'm fine, son," I said. "Looks really nice."

"Thanks. Okay." His jaw was doing its poking out thing. "This is the house we lived in. You and Mama helped us buy it. Look around. That bedroom, down the hall. That's where we slept. That kitchen, through there, that's where she cooked. Sometimes, I cooked. I made Swedish meatballs with pineapple. It was my specialty. She liked them. A lot. Through there, that's our yard. I was building a deck with a hot tub on it for her. She thought it'd be cool to sit in a hot tub when it snowed. Over there, that's where she planted a few crocuses and daffodils. So why, Deal? What the fuck did you think you were doing?"

I sank into that new sofa. I rested my elbow on the coffee table, closed my eyes, bowed my head, and held up my forehead with my hands.

"What can I say, son?" I lifted my head and looked up at him. He stood just beyond the coffee table. "I committed a terrible injustice, a sin I've been paying for from the moment... Look. I want you to hear me. I accept full responsibility. I let some silly flirtation go on 'til she moved in. I prepared the apartment for her to move in. I violated the sacred trust we had, you and me. I violated the sacred trust the whole family had in me."

I shook my head. "I can't tell you much more than that. We were never a couple if that gives you any peace. She lived in the same apartment with me, that's all, 'til she took off. We barely talked. I've never heard from her since. Don't care to."

Wally pulled a chair over and sat down.

"Son, I've always been a family man. In fifty-five years, that's who I've been, except… sometimes, the family was one I watching on TV. But I got plowed under. I don't expect you to understand. I didn't understand either until after your accident." In my mind's eye, I saw the plowed-under man bust out with his glowing tentacles creeping along, touching, touching. "I ceased being a family man for one minute of one day."

Hard as it was to do, I leaned over and touched his dear face. "It's almost impossible to understand, much less explain, but it felt like survival—a survival mechanism that had terrible repercussions. I hurt you all. I hurt you all deeply."

Wally stood up again and began pacing. Had I never noticed how compact he was? If his skin were darker, he'd look a lot like me.

"What do you mean survival? You didn't have to move out of your house, did you?" His fists were clenched. "You didn't have to rent an apartment, did you?"

"No, son, you're right. Some would have stayed in their home and lived with their transgression. Some might have gone so far as to carry on an affair and stayed home. I couldn't live with myself and Jonah at the same time after kissing another woman, your wife, just one time.

"I was arrogant enough to think Jonah would move out. Instead, she put me out. Had I been talking to Jonah, really talking for thirty years, there'd have been no moving. I wouldn't have been plowed under. There'd have been no transgression.

"Nice new sofa, son." I tried to change the subject, but Wally stopped pacing and was staring at me. I stood and forced myself to meet his eyes. "I am deeply sorry for the injury I've caused you, Wally. I'm deeply sorry for the injury I've caused Jonah and the rest of the family. I feel how cool they are. I see how angry you are. I know why. I do see why.

"But I'm still a family man, Wally. If anything, I know what a family man is now. I'm available in a way I don't think I've been before. Since I found you after the tractor accident..." My heart climbed into my throat, and I couldn't speak for a minute. "I'm available to love you if you can ever let me. I know that's probably way too much to ask. How would you know I wouldn't up and violate your trust tomorrow?"

"Yeah." His chin was going to town. "How would I know?" He moved the coffee table with his foot and stood right in front of me. "I want to come over to your apartment," he said. "You say you were never a couple. You swear on the Bible?"

"I swear, Wally," I said. "On everything holy."

"Then I want to walk through your apartment. I want to quit picturing her and you together in your apartment. I just want to see it for what it is."

"Okay," I said. "Okay."

Wally came over and walked through that basic but sad apartment where a lonely, middle-aged guy had been living. I think he saw it for what it is and for what it had been. He walked every inch of it, used the bathroom, stared at the bedroom a long time. All the while, he was shaking his head, like you do to exorcise the ghosts and demons that rumble around in there.

"You don't belong here," he finally said.

"C'est la vie," I said. "That's French."

He laughed. He seemed like he was going to put his arms around me but thought better of it and turned at the door. "Look," he said. "Our family needs to stick together. We need each other. But you ever betray me or anyone else in our family again, and I'll kill you. I will kill you, Deal. I won't mess it up either. You can pay for the tractor."

DAWN

I want to go back and torment everyone. I'm bored and lonely. I'm tired of hiding out in Kansas City, a couple of blocks from my mom's. I'm tired of working as a waitress on a casino boat. I serve hamburgers from noon 'til night. Then I go bar hopping 'til my namesake Dawn scratches her rosy fingers across the bleak mid-winter sky.

After the bar hopping, I catch forty winks and start all over again. Of course, guys flock to me like pheromones might become extinct. I can't help it. I don't *do* anything. They just arrive. I'm out with a different one every night. Wally, Deal, Field. Never got around to Daniel. I thought about giving Anna a try, but, hey, a girl's got to have some standards.

None of it means anything to me. I'm getting older, almost twenty-five. I sort of wish something meant something some of the time. I used to get off on just flirting and breaking people's hearts. But, hey, I've been flirting since I… never mind. Suffice it to say, it's been a while.

I think about Wally. He's the only one I ever married. Boy, was that a special day. He gave me $10,000 for the wedding and told me I could do whatever I wanted. I came in under budget too. I'd be good in business if someone would just give me a chance. I'm a good organizer and a good accountant. I have a flair for design. I'd be an asset to any company.

With the funds Wally gave me, I put together the most startlingly beautiful wedding day the Flint Hills has ever seen. I studied magazines and websites, and I wheedled with florists and caterers and dress shops 'til I got all the ingredients perfect. Also, I enlisted everyone in Wally's family to play a role, which they were eager to do once I had the basics worked out, so I had lots of help. Maybe I should be a wedding planner. Now that would be hot. Don't think the irony is lost on me. I'm not that dumb.

My dress was old ivory satin with a thousand teeny tiny buttons from the bodice to the hem. I had an ivory Alençon lace veil and a rhinestone tiara. The back of my dress was completely bare to the waist, and a pale rose train trailed behind with two of the nephews, Allen and Danny, to hold it to keep it from getting tangled. Marguerite was the flower girl, and Ivan was the ring bearer. They were adorable. The boys wore mini tuxes, and Marguerite had on a floor-length, calico summer dress with a scoop neck. Very innocent.

We were married in Wally's church. Anna and Alicia and I spent hours and hours making angels and doves the size of small lamp shades out of satin and wire. Some days, Jonah helped too. The guys hung them all over the church: in the main part where the ceremony was and in the social hall where we had our reception.

I had my hair styled back from my face with large curls cascading down behind, the way girls do for proms.

My flowers were a combination of white orchids and white daisies, for maturity and simplicity, qualities I could use more of, I suppose. I was hopeful, I guess, that by marrying Wally (and his family), I could gain a little more of both. It didn't happen. I got bored again and made a play for Papa Bear. What a disaster that was. Field should have fixed my pipes more often. That would have been a better choice. But he had to go all moral on me.

Now at the ripe old age of almost twenty-five, I'm heading along the path my sainted mother has worn so well.

I think about calling Wally or just dropping by. I could sneak into the house. I doubt he's changed the locks. I could just be sitting on the sofa we bought together, watching Oprah when he got home from work. I bet that would give him a start. I'd love to see the look on his face. But then again, he's got a bit of a temper. I don't know that I'd want to be there when I did see the look on his face.

Wonder whether he would consider taking me back? Mom said Alicia came by and wanted to contact me, wanted me to apologize to Wally and get Deal off the hook so the family could be "perfect" again, the way they used to be. Well, fuck that. Nobody's perfect. Obviously. Not even those salt-of-the-earth Strayhorns who took me in like I was one of them. Well, I showed them, didn't I? I showed them they were every bit as good as me. They came down to my level mighty quick. I guess that's where they'll stay. I'm not making it easier for them to commune or some shit. No point in me trying to go back. In two days of cleaning up the house and waiting for Wally to come home from work, I'd just be bored silly again. I guess I have gained some maturity after all. I can see ahead now. I can see that trying to reunite would be just one gigantic waste of my time. I think I'll e-mail Wally and let him file papers. Then I won't have to keep pretending to be incognito. I can start my wedding planner business. I'll be a divorcée wedding planner. How cool is that?

Chapter 38

JONAH

Sometimes, when you knit, you get a skein that has been wound so that the end of the yarn is obvious or just barely hidden. You unwind it a little from where it's tucked under itself. You pull, and the whole skein slowly unwinds itself from that one little tip of yarn. It's a very satisfying feeling. You can pay attention to the pattern you're knitting and know that each time you give a tug on the yarn, a little more will unwind. You will have the amount you need to knit until you get tired of knitting and cap off the needles and put the whole project away in your knitting bag

On other days, you'll get a skein that is wound up in a ball. Every time you pull an end, the ball rolls away from you, across the sofa, down the hall. The cat chases it and wants to play if you happen to have a cat. You need another pair of hands in the house to rewind the ball into a skein so it stays put. You try to set up a pair of chopsticks you've got left over from some take-out. You stick the chopsticks in the silverware holder in the dish drainer to serve as a pair of hands, and you try to rewind the ball around the chopsticks, but the chopsticks start leaning over and it's hard to wind the yarn evenly. You get mad and throw the chopsticks across the room. Nobody's home. Nobody can tell you to "Calm down, Mama, calm down." You get a pair of gloves out, stick them on the chopsticks, and stick the chopsticks in some old modeling clay. That works pretty well, but it makes you sad because you're winding the ball of yarn on some empty gloves. Where did all the hands go? I had four kids, but they grew up and moved away. I had a husband. He had a lot of nerve to *not* grow up and to move away. My mama would have happily sat in the kitchen with me, nursing a lukewarm cup of tea, sweetened by several pounds of sugar. She would have held up her hands for me most gladly and smiled.

When people see her photograph on the side table, they say, "Who's that, Jonah? She smiles just like you. Was that your mother?"

"That was my dear mother, Anna," I say proudly. "You think she looks like me?"

"Well," they hem and haw, "she smiles like you."

My mother was quite beautiful, striking like Anna. They don't want to say that I'm not beautiful, but the fact is well known. At least, my mother and I both inherited the mysterious smile that bound us, whether I was wrapping yarn around her hands or not.

I miss my dear mother every day. She died when I was sixteen. I never really knew my father except through her tales. Her translation of him. So I miss him more gently, like a lovely vapor you've smelled in the perfume aisle of a department store. You miss it for a moment, but then your eye is caught by the shoe display, and you forget to miss the aroma 'til later. Then you wish you'd just stood around inhaling a while before you moved on.

It's hard to watch your mother struggle. It's hard to watch your kids struggle and find there's not much you can do. You can't shape their lives for them. Goodness, you don't really shape your own.

It's as if that yarn I was talking about was deep inside of you. Someone invisible pulls on the end, and you blithely follow along. With Anna, I was afraid her yarn might be in a ball instead of a skein. I was afraid she'd go off to New York and roll around all over the place, never really focused, never really satisfied. I was just going to have to quit worrying. Turn her skein or ball or whatever over to her, over to each of us, and let our lives unravel as they would.

Chapter 39

ANNA

I was leaving Kansas City after a Saturday morning class when the heater in my 1991 Jetta started blowing foam all over me. I drove it to a gas station, got directions to a mechanic's where I could drop it off, and texted Milam to see if he could come get me. No reply, so I called Allie.

"Oh, you poor thing," she said. "Why on earth did it blow foam all over you?"

"How the hell would I know?" I grumped and then apologized, "Sorry, Al, not the best day."

"Hey, Field," she yelled, "mind if I run over to Kansas City to pick up your baby sister? Her car's messed up. Okay, kiddo, sure, I can come get you. How about I buy you lunch, and then we run get me some eyeliner?"

"Whatever," I said, still grouchy. "Sorry. I've got to get in a better mood. That would be great, Al. Sorry to put you out. I just have to get back in time to work tonight."

We ate a Tuscan salad at a bistro in Country Club Plaza and wandered around window-shopping and looking at the colorful tiles. "Allie," I said finally, "we better get your stuff 'cause I need to head on back."

We found an upscale cosmetics shop and were salivating at the almost sci-fi displays of colors and creams guaranteed to make us beautiful when we heard, "Well, well, well. Isn't it the little Miss Strayhorns, come to carry on the family name in style once again." Our heads practically wrenched off our shoulders we turned so fast.

"Dawn," Alicia gulped, "what a surprise." Dawn walked toward us from the back of the store. Her hair was pulled high in a tight bun, and she wore a snazzy teal suit with a rhinestone belt and spike heels.

"Not," I said.

"Tsk, tsk, tsk," Dawn said. "Haven't lost that famous spunk, have you, Anna? No reason to be so high and mighty. We seem to have something in common."

"You wish," I said.

"Asshole," Dawn said.

"Anna," Alicia pulled my arm. "Time to go."

"What's your rush? Let me sell you some product first. Didn't you come in for something?" Dawn continued.

"I just wanted some eyeliner," Alicia said.

"Color?" Dawn asked moving toward the counter again.

"Um, light brown, I guess." Alicia looked at me: do we stay or do we go?

"So how's the lovely Strayhorn family?" Dawn asked while setting out several very expensive eyeliners.

"Look, Dawn," I said. "We basically have nothing whatsoever to talk to you about. So if you don't mind, fuck off. We have to go."

"Hey, my name is still Strayhorn," she said coming out from behind the counter. "You can confide in me. Why'd you come all the way to KC to get eyeliner anyway? Trying some retail therapy after getting knocked up by your salt-of-the-earth father-in-law, huh, Alicia? Or maybe by your fixer-upper brother, Anna? Field's a good lay, you know."

Alicia's jaw dropped. "Why, you amazing bitch," she breathed.

I grabbed Dawn's well-tailored collar with my left hand and, POW, I planted a roundhouse punch squarely on her skillfully made-up face. Before we could make our rapid, possibly not so classy, exit, Dawn raked her perfectly shaped, stick-on, pearlescent fingernails across my left cheek, and one of them came off. Instinctively, I put my hand to my face to check for blood as Alicia pulled me out of the shop. "I've got a Kleenex in my purse," Alicia whispered. "Just let's get of here. I'll patch you up."

Alicia was hyperventilating, but sweet as she was, she placed a band-aid with Kermit's smiling face on my tender cheek. "What the hell was she talking about?" Alicia asked when we were safely ensconced in her SUV. "Why did she say that Field's a good lay?"

"I'm going to kill that hussy," I said. "Don't you know you can't listen to her? She'll say anything. She has no shame."

"Come on, Anna. What do you know?" Alicia prodded with great, gasping sobs. "You've got to tell me if you know something."

"Alicia, get real. She never spent time alone with Field. She's just got a filthy mouth, and she likes to rain trouble on—"

"—She did spend time alone with Field. Once he went over there to fix her pipes, the fucking bitch, when Wally was out of town."

"Goddamnit, Alicia. Field would not mess around. He loves you with all his heart."

“Yeah, he does.” Alicia agreed slowly. “But he’s a guy. He could have been susceptible.”

Chapter 40

DEAL

"You ran off with Dawn, didn't you, Grampa?" Ivan asked. My grandson, well, my adopted grandson from Manya's first marriage, was bubbling the liquid in a chocolate shake in the front seat of the pickup and looking at me over the top of his straw.

"Ran off with Dawn?" I was hoping to buy myself a little time. "Look, there's a copperhead," I said.

"Grandpa," he squinted at me. "That's a Great Plains Rat Snake."

"You're probably right, son." I took another look, but we were going too fast. "How did you know that?"

"I've got a book," he said. "At home. Mama got it for me when I was little. I can show you. You can color in it if you want. You have lots of snakes on the farm though. I can show you my list of all the snakes I've seen on the farm. Are you living back at the farm or did you still run off with Dawn?

I had my eyes trained on the road. No driving mishaps with my grandson, please.

"Turn right here, Grampa," he said pointing. What a little man, showing me how to get to Danny and Toto's daycare. "Why did you leave the farm, Grampa?" he asked again, still bubbling that shake.

"Did you ever have a perfectly good old bike?" I asked him, trying to phrase my question in terms he might comprehend, "but still want a shiny new one?"

Ivan mulled on that a bit. He took the top off the shake and peered inside to see whether there was any left or maybe whether there was any left to bubble. Then he looked up at me.

"Wouldn't Gramma let you have a shiny new bike? Doesn't she like you to ride bikes on the farm?"

He was quiet again. "Maybe if you promised her you wouldn't run over her flowers. Maybe she'd let you get a new bike and ride it on the farm."

"That's a good idea, Ivan," I said. "I'll ask her."

"Then you could go back to living there, and when I visit, we could hunt snakes together," he said. "Have you ever thrown a rock up at night and watched a bat swoop at it?" He had a tiny rubber ball in his hand and was throwing it up and catching it. The milk shake cup was at his feet.

"How about you show me how to do that?" I suggested.

"Okay," he said, "but you'll need to be at the farm so I can show you. It's not awful going there, Grampa, but Daniel just sits in the kitchen with Gramma, and Toto and Danny are just kids. It's more fun when you're there. I miss you, Grampa."

"I didn't know you felt that way, son," I said. It's hard to feel pride with your heart in your throat. "I miss you too, Ivan. I miss you too."

Driving back to the apartment, I heard Ivan's gentle voice echoing in my ears. "Why'd you leave the farm, Grampa?"

The moon was in a crescent and almost touching Venus like on some of those Muslim flags. I don't know why they get to have that picture on their flag. Like it's supposed to take the sky away from the rest of us.

Kind of like Jonah taking my family away from me. All my life, she was the center of the household. She wrapped herself around those kids 'til you couldn't tell where each left off from the other one. Spoiled them too much in my view. Didn't leave a place for me at all, except in that chair. That red leather chair. And then, came the grandkids, and she's back at it again. Enfolding everybody. Or at church, bringing the goodies, and everybody thanking her. And always cheery. Easy to be cheery when the money comes in regular, and you're not sweating it.

And if I worried and tried to get a little peace at night, what if I withdrew? Shouldn't she have cheered me up? Couldn't she bother to enfold *me* every now and then? Wasn't it up to her to keep my life from being empty? All the fields I've conquered. Year in, year out. Buy more land. Work harder. Be solvent even if no one else can make it.

My head hurt. At least, Ivan appreciated me. Course he's not even really kin.

Stop it, Deal. Stop griping. That's the old you. The new you cut a new life line, remember? The new you touched Wally's face.

SPRING
Chapter 41

JONAH

I'd been trying for months to get up the nerve to climb back into Deal's tractor or go down to the John Deere place. I had to find out whether my jabbing the screwdriver into Deal's tractor had caused Wally's accident. I needed to come to terms with what I'd done, but I was terrified to know the truth. What if I actually had caused the accident? How would I live with myself? What would I say to Wally?

Friday, I had the afternoon off, and I was sick of working in the garden. I'd tilled and planted and weeded and mulched 'til I thought I would scream if I even thought about mowing the yard. Funny, because I usually couldn't wait 'til winter abated, and I could get my hands in the dirt.

That afternoon, I had to go into the tractor shed for a pair of pliers, and I saw the very same screwdriver, or at least I think it was. But how could that screwdriver have gotten back on the tool rack? It had been dark that other time. It was pretty dim in there now. I just couldn't climb back into Deal's tractor. The thought of doing so flooded me with all the darkness of the past year.

Are you ready, Jonah? I asked myself. It's just a John Deere store.

Years ago, I would have put on a hat to go downtown, or at least my mother would have. I don't think I even own a hat now. I put on a skirt and blouse and some low-heeled sandals, brushed my hair, and got out a lipstick.

Although there weren't many customers ahead of me, I dawdled at the John Deere place, looking at the shiny green attachments, picking up a brochure here and there. No one asked whether I needed help. Apparently, it was up to me.

I moved to the rear counter at the parts section where two men were talking. They didn't even look up. "Excuse me," I finally said after shifting from foot to foot for several minutes and periodically patting my hair, "I'd like some information, please."

One of the men walked away. The other one looked at me. He had sandy hair. "I'm trying to find out about one of your tractors." My voice was weak. I hugged my purse to my side.

"What model?" The man asked.

"I think it's a 6430," I said.

"Now what would a little lady like yourself be wanting to know about a 6430?" The other man came back and picked a vise grip off the counter. He kept fiddling with the knob so the jaws got wider, then narrower. Really. Whatever happened to customer service?

"I know the tractor has a lot of safety features," I continued. "I think I dropped a screwdriver in the cab, and I just wanted to make sure it wouldn't malfunction the next time my husband took it out." I wondered whether these guys could see right through my tale. Maybe one of them was at that very moment pressing a button under the counter that connected directly to the police station. Maybe I'd be hearing sirens momentarily.

"Ma'am," the sandy-haired one said, "You can't really drop a screwdriver into it. I mean, you'd have to climb up into the cab."

"It was dark," I said with growing frustration. "I was hunting something in the tractor. I thought I knew where it was, so I didn't turn on the light. Then I dropped the screwdriver. I've been worried about it."

"Nothing to worry about," the sandy-haired man said. "If there was something to worry about, your husband would call us. He'd know right away if there was something to worry about."

"But, I mean, would it make a certain noise or something? Is that how he'd know?"

"Ma'am, has he used it since you dropped the screwdriver?" The sandy-haired man looked at the man fiddling with the vise grip.

"Well, yes," I said.

"And he was okay?"

"My husband is fine."

"See," the fiddling man spoke for the first time. "Nothing to worry about."

I wanted to scream at them, "Listen to me, you stupid, stupid men! Don't you understand that I wouldn't be here if it weren't important? I plunged the screwdriver into the tractor somewhere, and my son had an accident with the tractor not long after. Was it my fault?"

Instead of screaming, I took a deep breath and settled myself inside. I could feel my feet stretch in my sandals. "Harrumph," I said. I walked out of the building to the parking lot and looked up at one of the shiny, nine-foot tall tractors for sale. "Harumph," I said again for courage and hauled myself up the metal stairs to the tractor cab and opened the door. The fiddling man came running out after me, his buddy not far behind. I looked around the gleaming cab: knobs, dials, levers, screens. The immensity and complexity of Deal's life. None of it looked familiar from that night in the shed. That screwdriver could have stuck in a hundred places. Some looked open to serious damage; some not. Impossible to know definitively what I did or whether it contributed to Wally's accident.

"Ma'am, what do you think you're doing?" One of the men yelled up at me.

"I'm trying to figure out the answer to my question," I called back. "Neither of you seems to give a flip."

"Ma'am," he said again. "Please, come down. Ask me your question again. I'm all ears."

I looked around the cab again in the bright light of day, shook my head and sighed. The sandy-haired man held out his hand as I climbed down, but I didn't reach for it.

"Now please, ma'am, ask me again."

"The other night, in my husband's tractor, I kind of tripped in the cab. The screwdriver I was holding jammed into it somewhere. I want to make sure I did no serious damage to the tractor."

"More than likely not; I'd say ninety-nine percent likely not." The sandy-haired man spoke slowly and clearly. "But ma'am, if you don't know where you jammed it, we can't say for sure." He looked at his buddy, then back at me. "It'd be darn unlikely though, ma'am. Darn unlikely. That's one substantial machine."

Despite the fact that I might be interrupting Wally or he might not be in, I drove the interstate from the John Deere store to the industrial building where Field and Wally worked. I turned on the radio so I wouldn't think too much and change my mind. I had to talk to Wally now. When I knocked, he was munching a sandwich and staring at his computer.

"Mama," he asked, "what are you doing here?"

"Wally, I have to talk to you. I've done a terrible thing, a horrible thing. It's been on my mind for so long."

"Sit down, Mama. Sit down. How about a glass of water?"

I took a sip of that cool water, found a handkerchief in my purse, and dabbed a little water on the back of my neck.

"Wally, I think I caused your accident. Not long before you got hurt, I was in the tractor shed. I got so mad at Deal that day, I wanted to make a mark. I was so mad. I was so hurt. For me, for you, for all of us. I tried scarring his workbench, but it was already so marred, no one could tell I'd touched it. I climbed into the new tractor cab, and I jammed that screwdriver somewhere. I think I caused your accident, Wally. I've been wanting to tell you. I have to tell you. You have to know."

"Mama, Mama." He knelt down before me. "Mama, look at me. I saw a screwdriver when I was in that tractor. It was between the seat and the armrest. There was a slit there. I just thought maybe Deal stored it there in case he needed it. But I was going by the book that night, and I took it out and set it on the floor. It never hurt anything, Mama. It never had a chance to hurt anything. And here you've been worrying for nothing all this time."

"Are you sure, Wally? Are you sure?"

"Completely, Mama. Absolutely."

My shoulders relaxed. I think they'd been up to my ears. I hadn't even noticed.

"What was that prayer you used to say all the time when we were little?" Wally asked. "Something like, 'God, keep us safe.'"

"Please, God, keep us all safe. How did you know I said that? I never said it out loud. I just said it over and over in my head to hold you all...to keep you all from harm."

"I don't know, Mama. Maybe sometimes you didn't know you said it out loud."

"Please, God, keep us all safe."

"We're all safe, Mama. I love you, Mama. We're all safe."

WALLY

After Mama came by, I took some inventory of my own.

It had been weird visiting that apartment of Deal's where Dawn had been. Once I got up the nerve to go there, though, it was cathartic but anticlimactic at the same time. Afterward, the apartment stopped holding power over me. Before I went there, I would drive miles out of my way to avoid it, and now I could drive right by it unscathed—emotionally, I mean. I did run my car too near the curb one time when I was going by there a few weeks afterward, and I had to get a new tire. The sidewall was punctured, and it started leaking air.

I used to lie awake at night, night after night after night. I can't count the nights. I don't know how I was able to get through the days at work. This went on even after I started working for Field, even after I left Mama's and was helping Daniel out with the kids. Seemed like it went on forever. I went to work in a daze and came out the other side of the day, exhausted and still unable to sleep. I tried wine and booze, and they helped for a couple of hours or so. But a full night's sleep…forget it. I'd lie there, and these awful pictures of my dad making love to my wife would pound in my head. Like a jackhammer.

After I saw Deal's apartment and stopped being obsessed about how much sex had taken place there between my loving dad and my loving wife, I recovered another notch in the belt of my self-esteem.

I didn't even know if I believed Deal—that they had never had sex. I actually didn't believe it. But there was something about it I believed. Maybe they only had sex once or something, I'm not sure. But there was some truth to it. That apartment was too empty. It was awful. That furniture, my God. Like Deal had made it in his spare time out of scrap he scavenged at the dump. I don't know. Dawn would never have lasted in that place no matter how cool the guy. How hot the guy. Whatever. And she and I had had nice furniture. She picked it out herself, chrome and glass type stuff. I didn't care much for it. It wasn't my style. I liked antiques better. I guess the old worn stuff reminded me more of the homeplace. God, I had loved that house when we were young. Not that we had real antiques. Our house was actually pretty scruffy when I was a kid, with four of us running around, except for that unscuffed red leather chair, of course. Jesus. Come to think of it, I didn't notice that chair at Deal's when I went. Wonder what on earth happened to it?.

Why'd I choose her, I wonder? Why had it come to mean so much that she marry me and be happy?

I had all these conflicting feelings and thoughts now, lots of time to think, driving up to Daniel's after work, sitting home and watching TV. Hopped up on more coffee or some of that liquid jag stuff they sell now to keep you wired.

I felt like a sacrificial lamb. Like I was the Isaac to Deal's Abraham. I even went online to reread that Bible story. Actually, it made me feel worse than ever because in the Bible, although Abraham starts to do God's bidding and sacrifice his beloved son Isaac, his hand is stayed. God speaks to him before he goes through with killing Isaac, and he finds a ram in some kind of tree that he offers as a substitute sacrifice. Why didn't God offer a substitute for me to Deal? Why did Deal need to leave Mama in the first place? Why did he need a girl, a young girl at that, to leave her if he had to leave her? Why did he sacrifice me and my marriage? Why did he pick my wife? Why did she pick him? Ah, there's the rub.

So, as you can see, once I quit being tormented by images of sex between them, I was plagued instead by mountains of thoughts. Mostly questions. I didn't really want to ask Deal these questions again. I tell you I was sick of him. These feelings of wanting to reconcile but hating him and not wanting to reconcile.

My arm was working pretty well. A little soreness at times. A little stiffness at other times. They said I was lucky not to lose the arm. I'd quit limping. I made myself quit limping. The physical therapist said my alignment was good. "No reason to limp, Wally," he said. "Sometimes, you just have to remember what you were like before the accident and pretend to be whole again. Walk straight again. Then, slowly, your body will give up its desire to be handicapped. Bodies like pampering. Pamper your body for walking tall, and you will stop limping."

The guy should have been a preacher.

My head was okay too. Headaches if I watched too much TV or asked myself too many dumb questions about Dawn.

Otherwise, Field said I was a real catch...as an accountant. So there! Brain still worked. Columns and rows.

Now and then, I'd sneak off and go canoeing. I still loved being out there alone or with a crew. I loved feeling the paddle moving the water and feeling the boat adjust to a new position under my control. Well, my control along with the water.

Occasionally, Amanda, my SICU nurse, and I would take in a movie or go for a walk. I wasn't ready for anything more. Anna and I had become friends again. One day, she would make it to New York. I thought seriously about moving too. I decided it was time to contact an attorney and pay a visit to Dawn.

Dawn was unlisted, but her mother wasn't. Once I found her mother, it was too easy. Watch for Dawn to visit her mom. Follow her home.

Dawn lived in a condo, turned out. Not exactly astounding. Actually, she didn't seem all that surprised when I knocked on her door.

"What took you so long, Wally?" she said.

She looked tall, slim, and beautiful. She had on a caftan, I guess you'd call it. Very classy. A Turkish-type motif with gold braid around a plunging neckline. Her hair was glistening too, like she just brushed it, like she was expecting somebody. Perhaps she was.

"Quite the greeter, Dawn," I said. "Ever on your best manners."

"Can I get you something to drink?" she said. "Take off your shoes. Make yourself comfortable. I've got fifteen minutes. I've got a date."

"Shouldn't take that long, Dawn," I said. "Just sign on the dotted line."

"Fuck you, Wally," she said. "I'll show your papers to my attorney."

"Fine," I said. "You do that. How about you give your attorney fifteen minutes to send the documents back to my attorney."

She grinned. Maybe that's why I'd liked her. Down under all that crap of hers: lipstick and creams and the right car, there was somebody who laughed at my jokes. Other than someone who comes when you make love to them, or someone who makes other guys turn their heads, you can't get a better boost to your self-esteem than someone who laughs at your jokes.

I smiled at her. "You made a mess, Dawn. You hurt a lot of people."

"Yeah," she said. "I'm talented in that regard." She looked me straight in the eyes. She didn't look away.

"Why, Dawn?" I asked her.

"Shit, I don't know. Boredom? Because I could? I don't know. But, hey, I thought you were going to bust in here one day, hollerin', smashin' up the furniture. Whatever happened to your legendary temper?"

"It's a long story. Too long to tell in fifteen minutes. But you're right. That's what I would have predicted too. A long time ago."

"So are you dating anyone, Wally?" she asked. "You're looking good. Tanned. Buff." She tried a sloe-eyed look at me.

"Dawn, you know what?" I shook my head. "You never quit, do you? But I guess I'm finally immune." I took a good look at her, up and down. I looked around the room. Same type of chrome and glass furniture in the living room. Same type she picked out for our place. Not a lot of change of pace. I took it all in. When I got in my car for the drive back, I didn't want to have any more questions. I wanted to be done.

The whole way home I was shouting and singing loud to the radio and rapping on the steering wheel with my hand. I felt unplugged. I'd been plugged into a faulty socket that had kept zapping me, and now I was free. No more zaps. I'd been a drain line that was clogged up, and somebody had shoved a pole into it and unplugged the gunk that was way up in there. "I'm unplugged from Dawn," I kept yelling in the car to whoever was doing a commercial on the radio. "Come look at me; I'm unplugged from Dawn."

I called Anna on my cell. "Anna, I'm unplugged," I yelled.

"Hush up," she said. "You're busting out my eardrum. What are you so excited about, you idiot?"

"I already told you," I yelled again. "I'm unplugged. I went over to Dawn's in—"

"—What? You didn't? You can't have. You wouldn't."

"Anna, shut up and listen. Stop worrying. I went over there with divorce papers. Divorce papers. Hallelujah, hallelujah, I belong to the band, hallelujah. Divorce papers. D-I-V-O-R-C-E, will be final today."

"No. Get out. Divorce papers. Oh…my…God! Oh my God!" Now she was yelling. "Oh, Wally, get your ass up here. Come on, we'll celebrate. We'll raise our glasses to divorce."

I could see her pumping her fist in the air.

"Anna, I did it. I did it. I'm free, and I'm going to be free."

"Buddy, I'm sending you hugs all over the place."

"Hug you back, girl," I said. "I knew you'd be happy."

"Tell Alicia," she said. "She'll be happy too. Extremely so. Tell Alicia soon as you get a chance."

"Why Alicia?" I asked. "What's the deal with Alicia?"

"Trust me on this one," she said. "Call Alicia. Seriously."

"Alicia," I said. "Alicia?"

I didn't want to call Alicia. I preferred she get her news from Field. I could tell him when I got back to the office Monday. I could not imagine calling Alicia up and saying, "I've filed for divorce, Alicia. Thought you'd want to know. Anna said to call you." It was too awkward.

After our staff meeting Monday morning, I tapped Field on the shoulder and motioned with my head for him to go into his office.

"Wanted you to know I filed for divorce, Field," I said. "My marriage is over."

He started to say something, but all of a sudden, I just knew, kind of like with Deal. I knew. "Don't congratulate me, Field," I said. "Don't say, 'Hey, little brother, your marriage has been over a long time. Glad you're finally catching on.' Don't say any of that garbage. Dawn's available formally now. Not that formality ever got in your way. You want it, I'll give you her address. She's in Kansas City.

"And if you ever want to tell me why you betrayed me too, then please do. It might clear the air between us. Start a new beginning. Meanwhile, I'll be the accountant, and you be the boss. You want to be my brother again, you let me know. Ball's in your court." I turned and walked out.

He could tell Alicia tonight. She'd get her message. If she had suspicions, she'd have to work it out herself. Her and God and Field.

Chapter 42

JONAH

When Deal announced we were through, I put up no resistance. Probably because I always truly believed you couldn't change anyone else.

My friends in high school counted on changing their boyfriends. Stuff like: "He just needs a woman's touch to soften those rough edges," or worst of all, "I know he likes to play around now, but that'll all change when we get married."

I would try to tell them that you can't change anybody, but they wouldn't listen. One day when I was going through the salad bar line at lunch, it struck me. Have you ever seen any two people do their salad the same? One loves the pickled beets. One hates the pickled beets. One adds the pasta salad to the green salad and dribbles ranch dressing twice over the whole mess. Another sticks to LoCal and barely moistens the concoction enough to get it down. People are just set in their ways. There's no point in trying to slip a sunflower seed onto the salad of a bacon bits person.

So when Deal announced we were through, I didn't try to change him. Throughout our marriage, I was so busy staying in my own personal space so as not to violate his that I neglected to seek a bridge. Of course, he didn't seek a bridge either. A bridge to that red leather chair would have been a good idea. What might have happened had I unplugged his TV one night and proclaimed it "bridge" night? We could have taken a stroll or gone to a movie in town. He might not have welcomed it, but, more than likely, he would have gone along, and maybe we'd have begun to get the feel of each other once again. The feel of each other that gets under the skin. Where partners belong.

ALICIA

I'd never been a snooper. Stooping to snoop. Ha! Glad I still have my poetic sense of humor despite the fact that every cell in my body hurts. I've now stooped as low as the next human being and snooped in all Field's pockets and corners and come up with a goose egg. Zilch. So nothing left to do but confront him, and I am truly looking forward to that. Like a toothache. Like visiting my mother in her third rehab.

I waited 'til Friday when the kids could do an overnight with friends, and I put on a clean pair of cutoffs and a new summery top. I was working on a tan but hadn't quite got winter off my skin.

When Field walked in, he took one look at me and poured himself a drink. I fixed myself a gin and tonic, and we went out to the deck.

"So it's true?" I asked.

"So what's true?" he asked, buying time.

"So you had an affair with Dawn too?"

Long pause. I went in and got a box of Kleenex.

"Why, Field?"

He took a good swig and shook his head. "Beats me," he said. "There's no reason, no good reason, no reason that stands up in the court of love and justice. There's just stuff people do sometimes that is stupid and mean. Stuff they wish they could erase from their chalkboard. I'm a bastard, what can I say? There's nothing to say."

"Therapy," I said. "That's what there is to say. We're going to therapy to find out what we have together, and is it worth saving, is it salvageable."

"I can't go to therapy," Field said.

"You can't not go," I said. "Next Monday, 4 p.m. sharp. Here's the address."

Chapter 43

DEAL

I just can't get fire out of my mind. Every spring, I refresh the bluestem grass for our livestock with a prairie fire. I burn out all the woody, wooly weeds. I do it carefully. I've done it since I was a boy. Always after a rain. Always with help. We build firebreaks, places where we strip all the vegetation and make a small road so the fire is contained and can't get out of control.

Setting a prairie fire and then watching it burn is a seasonal ritual for our family, hell, for our whole community. You could say it was a metaphor for our way of life: a way to take control and burn down the obstacles in our path so spring could thrive. It's kind of like being God or, I know I shouldn't say this, better than God. Because we're making spring more abundant than God made her. Prairie fire had such an impact on our son Daniel that he's actually doing his dissertation on it.

What the family didn't know was that after I got back from Vietnam, particularly when the kids were little, I couldn't get satisfaction from the process any more. I couldn't get the same awe from the power of the blaze that I got as a boy. In fact, the whole idea of setting this massive fire scared me and reminded me of napalm fires I'd seen set or newsreels of children running, burning, their skin melting off.

I didn't like feeling scared. I wasn't used to it. Even in Vietnam, I don't remember feeling much fear. Well, maybe sometimes. But at least in Vietnam, I was with my buddies. I was there to get a job done and get back to the farm, God willing. When I did get back to the farm, Vietnam stayed with me for a long time. The jungles would come and sit themselves down on top of a field while I was plowing it. That can be a mite unnerving.

Eventually, Vietnam faded except for now and then. A field became just a field. I even got where I could appreciate that the prairie fire I set was working for me. Even though I never really was totally free of associating the fire with fear, I could at least appreciate its effectiveness.

Now, though, I feel like I'm getting obsessed with fire in a different way. Daniel called me the other day and wanted me to let him know when I was going to set the fire this year. He wanted his kids to come and watch. He was going to call Field too and see if Field wanted his kids to come watch. I think Daniel's trying to recreate his childhood. He remembers when Jonah would make sandwiches for all the neighbors and cocoa for the kids after everyone helped out and had a chance to wash up. I think Daniel's trying to recreate one big happy family. Can't say as I blame him, but somehow the idea of fire gets me all stirred up in a rage. I just want to let the fire get out of control and burn everything down. I almost think I'm going crazy.

Shoveling hay for the cattle, I'll be checking the wind to see how much damage a fire would do if I set one right here and now. Would it endanger the animals I've spent my life tending? Would it endanger the crops? Would the fire make it down to the house? Would Jonah burn up in that house and quit haunting me?

That's really what it's about, isn't it? I'm so mad at Jonah, I want her to burn in hell because I'm stuck in that awful apartment and can't have my home back; I can't have my wife back; I can't have my family back. That's what it's all about, this obsession with fire. I must be going crazy. More and more, I'm blaming Jonah that I can't get my life back. Yeah, yeah, I know I started it, but she could finish it. She could make it all better. And she won't.

Chapter 44

ANNA

Daniel and I brought the kids down from Lawrence to watch the prairie fire. Milam was on a project out of town. Alicia came with Marguerite and Allen. Jonah was in the kitchen making a slew of sandwiches and a vat of cocoa, like in the old days. Just a different crop of kids now, watching the final preparations, hardly able to contain their excitement. Daniel was holding Toto in his arms and giving him a bottle. He'd drink from a cup during the day, but toward evening, he was still eager for the comfort of a bottle. Deal hovered on the sidelines, I think to get closer to all of us, as close as he thought he was allowed. Field and Wally…I don't know. I guess they decided they'd seen enough fires.

Deal gave the signal, and two of his helpers lit the weeds on either end of the field. The whole row must have been primed because fire whooshed all the way across—the way a grill does when you just light one part.

It was dusk, and the fire flared bright against the fading light. It began to advance, crackling, then roaring. In the smoke, you could see pictures, like in a cloud formation. A genie in a bottle, a dragon, figments of your imagination you couldn't name before they changed into something else entirely.

All of a sudden, Danny darted toward the flames as fast as his little legs could go. Daniel couldn't move fast enough with Toto in his arms. Alicia grabbed her kids. I grabbed Ivan.

Jonah must have still been in the house. Deal must have been distracted for a second because Danny kept getting closer and closer to the flames. When Deal looked up, he sped after Danny so fast I thought he might have a heart attack.

I couldn't quite see whether Danny's hair or his clothes had caught fire. Deal grabbed him and raced back behind the firebreak.

Danny was struggling with Deal and hollering, "Let me go. Let me go. I saw Mama. Mama's in the fire. Mama's in the fire. I want to go to Mama. Let me go. Let me go."

Deal pushed Danny to the ground as gently as he could and covered Danny with his own body to snuff out any remaining sparks. Danny's cries were muffled, but he banged on Deal's chest with his tiny fists.

By that time, Daniel had handed Toto to me and rushed to Danny and Deal. "Danny, Danny, Danilushka. Are you okay? What were you thinking? Are you okay?"

Deal lifted himself off Danny but held him fast while he looked him over. Everyone had reached them, but Deal told us to get back and give Danny air. The fire continued its course with Deal's helpers monitoring its progress.

Danny's face was streaked with tears and ashes. His hair smelled singed and had frizzed up at the edges.

"You stink," Ivan said.

"Hush, Ivan." Jonah had run out of the house, apron flapping. "Ivan, get Danny a drink of water. Anna, go draw him a cool bath. Quick," she said, taking Toto from me.

Stripped down, Danny looked so pitiful, and he started to cry again. "I saw Mama. I saw her out there. I want my mama."

"I know you do, sweetheart," I washed him gently, checking he didn't have any burned places that would need medical attention. "I know you do. I miss her too. We all miss her terribly. What a good Mama you had. She loved you so.

"I saw pictures in the fire, Danny," I said. "Just like you did. And in the smoke too. But those are just pictures, honey. They are just pictures we make with our mind as the fire changes shape. Those pictures aren't real. But your mama was real when she was alive, honey. And she's real now in your heart. I don't mean like a person is actually in your heart. But her love is in your heart."

"What do you mean, her love is in my heart?"

"Remember? I told you before. It's a feeling. It's like a feeling and a memory all wrapped up into one. The person you love who loves you can never ever leave you. Her love is in your heart. It will always be in your heart. Always and forever."

Chapter 45

WALLY

Field and I worked late the night of the prairie fire. The lawsuit over Manya's death was still being prepared, but the lawsuit against Field was supposed to go to trial next week, and we were going over our case with our attorney. I say "our." Funny, Field made me a partner in Strayhorn Enterprises. I don't work for Mayfield Strayhorn any more. We work for ourselves and each other now.

Our attorney was cautiously optimistic about the outcome. He said we were in the right. Our actions were all well documented. "But you never know what may happen in court," he said. "Stay positive, but be ready for anything."

Alicia interrupted our discussion with the attorney when she called Field about Danny. As soon as Field realized what had happened, he put her on speakerphone so I could hear. "Danny's just fine," she told him. "I trimmed a little of his hair, and Anna bathed him and shampooed him a few times to get the smell out. He'll be just fine. Physically anyway. I wonder, though, whether he should go to a therapist…with Daniel and Ivan maybe. Obviously, he's hurting so bad about losing Manya. What do you think?"

"What do you think, Wally?" Field turned to me.

"Jees, I don't know," I said. "Do they ever do any good? I always thought they take your money and run. I thought about going when Dawn left, but I left the idea in the trash. I never went. Have you ever gone, Field?"

"Alicia and I have been going lately," he whispered. "We have some stuff to work out. Don't worry, bro. We're working on it. We're going to work it out."

"Good," I said. "That's good. I really like Alicia."

"Me too," Field said louder, so she could hear, "I really like Alicia too."

"We can talk about the therapy thing later," Alicia continued, "but listen, Field. When Deal saved Danny, he covered him with his own body. They were way down the field, and I couldn't see great with all the smoke. Plus, it was getting dark. I was hanging on to our two for dear life, but it looked like Deal might have gotten burned when he turned his back on the fire and carried Danny away. We were so busy taking care of the kids, especially Danny, next time we looked, Deal's helpers were tending what was left of the fire, and Deal had gone. Maybe you should call him, Field," she said. "Check up on him."

"I need to call him, bro." Field glanced at the attorney we'd been working with. Poor guy looked a little green around the gills.

"I'll call him," I said. "You finish up here. I'll call him."

"Deal, where are you? We heard you might have been hurt rescuing Danny."

"Wally? Hi, son. I'm in the ER. Just some minor burns on my back. My shirt stuck to my back, and I didn't want to rip it off, so I thought I'd better drop by here on my way home. They're going to fix me right up. Nothing serious. Nice of you to call though."

"I'm coming over there." I started gathering up my sweater, a half empty bag of chips, some papers. "I'll be there in a minute."

"No need, Wally. I'll be fine. Truly."

"Quit being so macho, old man," I said. "Haven't you learned anything yet?"

"Whew," Deal exhaled. "Okay, Wally. Fine then. Whatever you say."

Deal had burned a respectable-sized patch of skin on his back when he blocked Danny from the flames. "Second-degree burns, it looks like." The nurse was matter-of-fact. "We'll get him fixed up. Dress that burn. Give him an antibiotic and something for the pain. Good thing he didn't try to take that shirt off himself. Sounds like he's a hero, huh? Saving his grandson like that? Quite a guy."

"Yeah," I grinned at Deal. "Quite a guy."

Chapter 46

ANNA

It was on toward early summer when Daniel defended his dissertation successfully and had time to interview prospective nannies. Jonah took a week's vacation and accompanied me to New York. On the plane, she hesitantly asked me about Milam.

"I love him, Mama," I said. "But I have to give this a try. I have to find out whether I can make it as a dancer. Soon, it will be too late.

"I told him at my favorite coffee shop that I had to go. I think he understands. He's going to try to find a job in New York. He maybe wants to go to architecture school. We'll see what happens, but I've got to give this a try."

I leaned my head back on that little cloth they have on the back of the seat in the plane and thought about the last time I met Milam at the coffee shop.

"I like you a lot, Anna," he said and took my hand. He lightly stroked my hair and let his finger trace the side of my face. "It's your spirit. And the smile. It's the kindness. It's your nose. I think it must be your nose although it's a little red at the moment. Also, the chocolate on the side of your mouth."

"At first," I said, "I thought you were just going out with me to help your dad get in with my mother."

He took a napkin and dabbed it in his water glass and wiped the corner of my mouth. "You are one insane person," he said. "So confident and trusting. That's what I like most about you." He shook his head. "But watch out. I'm very fickle. Tomorrow, I may like something else about you. And I'm very mercenary. I understand you have a big family. Tomorrow, instead of seeing you so my dad can sneak into your mom's good graces, I might see you so I can have a fling with Daniel."

"But you don't even know Daniel," I protested and saw that he was laughing. "Now you're making fun of me," I said blushing.

"Because you are funny." He kissed me on the corner of my mouth. "I shouldn't have wiped the chocolate off," he said.

JONAH

Anna used our forced confinement on the plane to ask me a few intimate questions too.

"Mama, Do you believe they slept together?"

"Who, honey?" I asked, still wrapped up in her life.

"Mama! Deal and Dawn, damnit. Don't make me spell it out."

Anna started to cry from deep down in her belly like you do when you're a little girl, and you've been blamed for breaking one of your brother's toys, and you're innocent.

"Come here, honey." I moved the armrest up into its slot and pulled her toward me.

"Anna, people are just human. It's not like this is easy for anybody, me included. Believe me. I was so mad one night when I went in the tractor shed for a screwdriver that I drove that screwdriver into the tractor somewhere."

"Mama!" She lifted her head off my shoulder, sniffled back her tears, and stared at me.

"So I've been mad," I continued. "I've been devastated. All of us have been. But it doesn't help to lie to ourselves, does it?

Of course, they slept together. And then, despite all his virility and charm, she left. Now,] he's devastated too, like the rest of us. I don't think he misses her that much. He misses us."

"Mama, I love you." Anna shook her head. "You're not exactly how I thought you were, you know? I can't believe you stuck a screwdriver in his precious tractor."

"I love you too, honey," I said.

She looked so small then. I remembered her in a pinafore on Easter Sunday with a broad-brimmed hat with two ribbons hanging down and patent leather Mary Janes with silk socks with lace around the ankles. It was like yesterday, the memory was so strong. But I wasn't born yesterday.

Anna had found a fine apartment online in Brooklyn, with two crazy-looking roommates. One had spiked hair dyed a red that made me smile every time I saw it. A red like the foil they put around poinsettia plants at Christmastime. She was a girl, technically, with dark eyeliner, very thin. An aspiring dancer too. The other was a guy, possibly a homosexual would be my guess from his voice, also a dancer. Very willowy, although I suppose he had to be muscular to lift the female dancers. They were both lovely to us. They told Anna and me where to hunt for basic furniture for her room, and they helped us move it in and arrange it. They drew maps for Anna, dissected dance schools for her, and gave me subway directions for museums while she was job-hunting.

New York is a wonderful place. You can walk around and look...at a vegetable store. At home, you go to the grocery store to buy your vegetables. You don't look at them. You might if you go to a Farmer's Market. New York is like a Farmer's Market. You look at everything. You can pick up a bunch of cherries the way you did when you were a kid, looking for the pair that might still be attached at the stem, that you could hang over your ears like earrings.

I know there's a seamy side. We saw drunks passed out in corners, and we saw homeless people sleeping on cardboard. It's just that your eyes are alive in New York. I liked that feeling. I decided that when I go home, I will remember to get my eyes alive every day.

Anna suggested I take a yoga class or meditate. I don't know. I might just conjure up my own way of raising my eyelids a little wider when I find I've gone back to sleep inside. It might be a little harder back home. Everything is so familiar. That just means it'll be more of a challenge. It'll be good for me.

Chapter 47

DEAL

I don't know who I am any more with all these different moods. One minute, I'm dreaming of letting the fire get out of control to kill Jonah. The next minute, I'm saving my grandson from the same fire. I might as well be Anna when she was in high school. Or maybe I've been going through some kind of male menopause if they have male menopause.

Strangely enough, after I got back to my apartment, the day of the fire, I felt a sensation I had not experienced in a long, long time. I felt proud of myself. I hadn't realized just how much I'd missed feeling proud. I used to enjoy at least a sense of accomplishment every day when I was taking care of the farm for my family. I suppose that's where I got my identity. Just like a woman does when she takes care of her family, cooking and cleaning. A man needs to be taking care of his family to be a man. Or at least I need to.

Feeling proud, I felt more like the Deal I'd been looking for. I wasn't angry at Jonah any more. I wasn't blaming her. I was standing up like a man. I had stood up like a man. I could raise my head again. Funny, it wasn't the preacher and the congregation who had tormented me for my sins all these months. It wasn't even Jonah who couldn't forgive me. It was me. I can quit holding onto her mother's silver pin. I can take it back. It belongs to her. I can always grab a buckeye next fall and hold onto it if I need something to hold on to.

Pride in my pocket and hair washed clean from the day's planting, I checked and double-checked that I did indeed have Jonah's mother's pin polished up and wrapped like a present on the truck seat beside me. I felt the same nerves I felt at eighteen. Friday night. Too scared to call Jonah and prepare her for my visit. She might not be home. She might be out on her walk. Or visiting one of the kids. Or out on a date.

Please, God, don't let her be out on a date.

JONAH

I don't know what it was after I got back from New York: spring, the passage of time, what. But it wasn't just my eyes that were open wide. My body opened to these fine, light mornings like a flower. Sometimes, I wanted to embrace the day, all in a rush, but mostly, I was aware of a sensual awakening that was very delicate. It was like my nipples were reaching out to the morning air, stretching with a yawn. My fingertips resonated with the vibrations of the old dishwasher. My gums tingled when I brushed my teeth.

I was anticipating the ripening of my heirloom tomatoes, firm and warm in the sun. When you bite into one, your teeth pierce the taut skin, and your mouth revels in expectation. I often take a salt shaker out to the kitchen garden with me. After the first bite, I sprinkle a little onto the tomato. The next bite will be totally perfect. As perfect as life can get. A hint of salt on the sweet tomato meat. The firm skin. My breasts get a little rounder knowing what summer will bring.

What was a respectable woman in my condition to do? I could become less respectable, but that didn't seem to fit. I couldn't really grow younger either when all would have been forgiven as experimentation. Funny, part of me didn't want to share these feelings with anyone. But part of me wanted to hold and be held. Part of me wanted to lie down in the sweet earth with a dear lover and get dirt all over my body and his body and then get in a steaming shower and rub him with a thick, plush towel. I didn't have any thick, plush towels though. They were mostly cheap to start with and worn thin with use.

After a few days of this flowering feeling, I went to the specialty bath shop downtown and bought six luxury towels in different hues and placed them on the towel racks. That just made it all worse. They were so inviting.

I thought about going out with Hollis, but I balked at the possibility like an old mule. That idea was going nowhere. The person I most wanted to be my lover was Deal. I didn't want to be married any more or at least not in the same way as before. But I wanted to be with him. I wanted to be beautiful with him.

I could see letting Deal build a cabin on the other end of the farm and visiting him sometimes. When I thought about it, I saw that cabin inching, day by day, closer to the farmhouse like a puppy in training, edging closer to a treat without permission. The picture of the cabin moving closer didn't make me flinch. I welcomed it. I knew Deal would like living back on our land more than any place else in the world.

I planted two rows of broccoli and cabbage, sat back, and took off my gardening gloves to run my fingers through the warm, rich earth. As I started on the third row, I heard a vehicle approaching on the drive.

Deal got out of his truck and looked in all directions before he spotted me.

"Jo," he called out. "Jo." He ran toward me. "Jo." I rose. "Jo." I reached out my hand. "Jo." Deal knelt before me on bended knee and put a wrapped box in my hand. "It fell out of the red leather chair," he said.

I took the box, looked at the wrapping, and knelt down beside him. I set the box on the ground, and I put my arms around him. He buried his face in my hair. I could smell the wild prairie roses just starting their season along the garden fence. He lifted his head and looked at me. He stroked my cheek and fingered a smudge of dirt. I looked back at him, eyes wide. I smiled.

Thanks to:

Jeff, Adam, Eli, and Courtney Tiller
Frederick, Anny, and Michael Wiener Kraus
Sally Farmer
Bette Ruth Hanson
Vann Joines
Barbara Massar
Susanna Stewart
Eileen Walbert
High Country Writers
The Name of the Rose
Monday Writers Group
Sandy Horton
Greg Adams, MD
Tré Easterly
Jon D. Pool, CPA
Paula Taylor, RN, PhD, CAN
Marc Goodman, DA
Sue Smith
T.J. Hittle
Danko Sipka
Silvija Sturgalve
Lyon County Historical Society
Derrick Bam
Antonio Amor, M.D.
Irina Barclay
Brian Rees
Lauren Whaley
George Ude
Murray, Stuart, *Eyewitness Vietnam War*, New York: DK Publishing, 2005.

About the Author

Ingrid Kraus is a writer and psychologist. She lives with her husband, Jeff Tiller, in the mountains of North Carolina. You can find her short stories in the anthologies, *High Country Headwaters* and *Drowning Allison and Other Stories*: http://www.tinyurl.com/dr-al-oth-st.

www.ingramcontent.com/pod-product-compliance
Lightning Source LLC
Chambersburg PA
CBHW030107070426
42448CB00036B/317

* 9 7 8 0 6 1 5 7 2 3 7 0 9 *